HERBERT HOOVER'S
Challenge to America
His Life and Words

By the Editors of COUNTRY BEAUTIFUL

Editorial Direction: Michael P. Dineen

Edited by Robert L. Polley

Published by Country Beautiful Foundation, Inc., Waukesha, Wisconsin

Distributed by Doubleday & Company, Inc., Garden City, New York

COUNTRY BEAUTIFUL

Publisher & *Editorial Director:* Michael P. Dineen

Executive Editor: Robert L. Polley

Art Director: Robert W. Pradt

Managing Editor: Charles R. Fowler

Senior Editors: Kenneth L. Schmitz, James H. Robb

Art Assistant: Robert Fehring

Staff: Sharon L. Griswold, Vicki Russi

COUNTRY BEAUTIFUL Magazine is published by Country Beautiful Foundation, Inc., 24198 W. Bluemound Rd., Waukesha, Wis., a nonprofit organization dedicated to strengthening and preserving the physical, cultural and moral values of America and other nations of the world.

The Editors are grateful to the following publishers for permission to include copyright material in this volume: The Caxton Printers, Ltd. for excerpts from *Addresses Upon the American Road (1955-1960)* by Herbert Hoover. ©1961 by Herbert Hoover. Coward-McCann, Inc. for excerpts from *Shall We Send Our Youth to War* by Herbert Hoover. ©1939 by Herbert Hoover. Reprinted by permission of Coward-McCann, Inc. D. Van Nostrand Company, Inc. for excerpts from *Addresses Upon the American Road (1941-1945)* by Herbert Hoover. Copyright 1946, D. Van Nostrand Company, Inc., Princeton, N.J. D. Van Nostrand Company, Inc. for excerpts from *Addresses Upon the American Road (1945-1948)* by Herbert Hoover. Copyright 1949, D. Van Nostrand Company, Inc., Princeton, N.J. Doubleday & Company, Inc. for excerpts from *Hoover Off the Record* by Theodore G. Joslin. Henry Regnery Company, Chicago, Illinois, for excerpts from *An American Epic* by Herbert Hoover. Copyright ©1959 by Herbert Hoover. The Macmillan Company for excerpts from *The Memoirs of Herbert Hoover: The Years of Adventure* by Herbert Hoover. Reprinted by permission of the Macmillan Company. Copyright, 1951, by Herbert Hoover. The Macmillan Company for excerpts from *The Memoirs of Herbert Hoover: The Cabinet and the Presidency* by Herbert Hoover. Reprinted by permission of the Macmillan Company. Copyright 1951, by Herbert Hoover. The Macmillan Company for excerpts from *The Memoirs of Herbert Hoover: The Great Depression* by Herbert Hoover. Copyright 1952, by Herbert Hoover. Reprinted by permission of the Macmillan Company. McGraw-Hill Book Company for excerpts from *The Ordeal of Woodrow Wilson* by Herbert Hoover. Copyright ©1958 by Herbert Hoover. Used by permission of McGraw-Hill Book Company. William Morrow and Company, Inc. for excerpts reprinted from *On Growing Up* by Herbert Hoover. Copyright ©1949, 1959, 1962, by Herbert Hoover by permission of William Morrow and Company, Inc. Random House, Inc. for excerpts reprinted from *Fishing for Fun — And to Wash Your Soul.* Copyright ©1963 by Herbert Hoover, compiled by William I. Nichols, by permission of Random House, Inc. Charles Scribner's Sons; used by permission of Charles Scribner's Sons: Extracts from *America's First Crusade* (Copyright 1941 The Curtis Publishing Company, Inc. Copyright 1942 Herbert Hoover), *The Challenge to Liberty* (Copyright 1934 The Curtis Publishing Company, Inc. Copyright 1934 Charles Scribner's Sons; renewal copyright ©1962 Herbert Hoover) and *Hoover After Dinner* (Copyright 1933 Charles Scribner's Sons; renewal copyright ©1961 Herbert Hoover).

Grateful acknowledgement is made to the following, without whom this book would not be possible: Dr. Rita R. Campbell, Archivist and Research Associate, the Hoover Institution on War, Revolution, and Peace; Joseph T. Radel, Forest Supervisor, Forest Service, U.S. Department of Agriculture; Henry Scharer, Director, Office of Public Information, U.S. Department of Commerce.

John J. Kosmitis

Hoover Tower at Stanford University, California.

CONTENTS

PREFACE

HERBERT HOOVER : A Personal View

My warm and close friendship with President Herbert Hoover dates back to the day he visited Washington, shortly after I succeeded to the Presidency.

I was never among those who held President Hoover accountable for the economic disaster of the late 20's. And, while I did not see eye to eye with him on many of the basic domestic and foreign issues, I have held him in high respect as a devoted public servant and a great humanitarian.

It was in this higher calling that I was moved to invite him back into public service in the hope that he might resume the task of again feeding the hungry, in the wake of the frightful devastation visited on so many human beings in many parts of the world. I wanted to help restore as quickly as possible friend and foe alike to their normal lives and to peaceful pursuits.

President Hoover did not hesitate, nor did he weigh the matter of personal convenience and even hardships. He accepted at once. The meeting between him and me at the White House is now history. His work in feeding the hungry expressed the care and generosity of all Americans, regardless of political differences.

President Hoover and I have visited each other frequently and whenever either of us happened in the neighborhood of the other, we felt free to just drop in.

President Hoover helped in the dedication of the Library in Independence, Missouri, and I was glad to take part in the dedication of his Library at West Branch, Iowa. Briefly put, he was my friend and I was his.

Harry Truman

HARRY S. TRUMAN
INDEPENDENCE, MISSOURI
June 1965

The Burlington tracks in West Branch, Iowa, along which Herbert Hoover hunted for agates as a boy.

Introduction

A PROFILE OF INDIVIDUALISM

In the indelible pages of American history, the name Herbert Hoover appears destined for eternal association with national economic disaster. However unjust, the chronicles of time judge a man at the zenith of his achievement in life. For Herbert Clark Hoover, history's harsh judgement was pronounced after the 1929 stock market collapse plunged the nation into economic depression, only nine months after his inauguration as President of the United States.

Historians seldom fail to record that the 31st President was an unfortunate victim of fate. "Mr. Hoover was hardly more responsible for the downfall of business hopes of the nineteen-twenties than for the invasion of Belgium [by the Germans in 1914]," one journalist observed. But the nation that cheered Hoover as the administrator of Belgian food relief during World War I turned its back on his recovery efforts as President after the economic crisis of 1929.

The imprint of recent history is vivid in the minds of many who stood in breadlines during the nation's last major depression. Only the passage of time has sufficiently dimmed emotion-charged memories to permit a more meaningful view of Herbert Hoover — his purpose, his courage, his achievement.

Born of Quaker parents in West Branch, Iowa, on August 10, 1874, Hoover's boyhood provided a stringent moral foundation for his long life. His father was a mechanically-minded blacksmith; his mother a kindly, religious woman with fundamental beliefs. Both parents contracted illnesses common to the period and Hoover was orphaned before reaching his tenth year.

In the family of a benevolent uncle, young Hoover moved to Newberg, Oregon, at the age of eleven. Growing up in the rapidly expanding West, his sphere of experience increased, but he retained the characteristic shyness which one biographer called the "crown" of his personality.

With savings of $300, Hoover enrolled with the first class at California's Stanford University in 1891 to prepare for a career in geology and engineering. Among his fellow students, he was remembered more for his ordered, business-like daily life than for his

A wood near West Branch as it appears today.
Hoover often recalled his boyhood activities in Iowa woods.

Phil McCafferty

shy, unassuming manner. To stretch his meager savings, the young student started laundry and newspaper routes, was student assistant to a professor and spent his summers as a land surveyor.

Graduating with a degree in mining engineering in 1895, Hoover found jobs extremely scarce in the depression that followed the economic panic of 1893. The young engineer finally found an opening as a $2.50 a day pick-and-shovel laborer in California's ore-filled Sierra Nevada mines. His months as a miner provided valuable practical experience and he was soon hired by a noted San Francisco mining engineer. With characteristic precision, Hoover added management skills to his theoretical and practical background.

When only 23 years old, Hoover was sent to Australia to organize and manage a newly discovered gold mine. Within months the young engineer-manager pushed the project to completion. His success brought an offer from the Chinese government to serve as a consultant to its inefficiency-plagued mining operations. Once again Hoover molded men and materials into an efficient organization.

During a return trip to the United States in 1899, Hoover married Miss Lou Henry whom he met while at Stanford. In the twenty years that followed, the couple made extensive business-connected visits to China, Europe, Russia, Southeast Asia and

The house in Newberg, Oregon, where the orphaned Hoover
lived with relatives after leaving Iowa at the age of eleven.

Africa as Hoover acquired mining interests throughout the world. A millionaire businessman at 40, Hoover saw his mining organization collapse when the naval blockades of World War I cut sea transportation lines between his mines and industrial markets. But the difficulties of war carved out a new career for the successful administrator-manager.

The assassin's bullet which catapulted Europe into the First World War caught many American visitors abroad without the means to return home. Hoover was called in by President Woodrow Wilson's administration to organize the huge civilian transportation effort. No sooner had he completed his task than he was asked to lead the more difficult relief program to feed millions of starving Belgians trapped between the advancing German army and the Allied shipping blockade which cut off all food shipments. As administrator of Belgian relief, Hoover tapped private and government resources in many nations and then met face-to-face with both enemy and Allied leaders to persuade them to cooperate in the humanitarian program. His planned, voluntary effort was an unqualified success and Hoover, the engineer of human relief, gained personal stature on all continents.

Refusing compensation for his work, Hoover continued to serve in relief positions during the war, as Food Administrator in the United States and finally as Chief of the Supreme Allied Economic Council.

Although a member of the Wilson administration at the end of the war, Hoover aligned himself with the Republicans early in 1920. Hoover's longtime friend and biographer, Will Irwin, wrote that as a young boy in Iowa, Hoover had been weaned on Grand Old Party politics. "He had been brought up in a town which included one Democrat; the principles of the Republican Party were . . . as much a part of [him] as his religion . . ." Always a proponent of "rugged individualism," Hoover found a measure of philosophical harmony in Republican politics.

Hoover became Secretary of Commerce in the administration of President Warren G. Harding. He won the cautious support of Congressional and business leaders by streamlining department operations and promoting voluntary cooperation between business, industry and labor. Seven years as a progressive, respected cabinet member paved the way for greater responsibilities. When Harding's successor, Calvin Coolidge*, announced he "did not choose to run" for a second full Presidential term in 1928, Republican leaders turned to Hoover as their standard bearer. He was nominated by the national convention at Kansas City, Missouri, on June 14, 1928.

Hoover's Democratic opponent for the Presidency was New York Governor Alfred E. Smith. The campaign issues revolved around prevailing prosperity, prohibition, the tariff and farm relief. A less noble, but politically significant factor, was that Governor Smith was the first Roman Catholic to be nominated for Presidential office. The prosperity theme, carried to bandwagon proportions in the Republican campaign, appeared to prevail as voters went to the polls. On November 6, the vote was tallied and Herbert Hoover was elected President by a six million vote landslide.

---

* Vice-President Calvin Coolidge succeeded Harding as President after Harding's death in San Francisco on August 2, 1923. He was elected to a full Presidential term in 1924.

With Hoover's inauguration on March 4, 1929, the nation looked forward to a continuation of Coolidge prosperity with Hoover adding his promised "chicken in every pot." Nine months later the nation's paper prosperity collapsed. After years of postwar laissez-faire speculation, the stock market crashed at the feet of financial Titan and sugar bowl investor alike. In its darkest hour, the nation looked to the White House — to a man world-renowned as a financial expert and an administrator of human relief — for leadership toward recovery.

Hoover reacted quickly to the nation's economic crisis. Although clouded in historical obscurity, Hoover was the first President to use limited executive powers to counter a depression. Two other chief executives, Presidents Grant in 1873 and Cleveland in 1893, let depressions run their course without positive intervention.

As President, Hoover promoted individual initiative and private voluntary cooperation to lead the nation's recovery. He hesitated to extend the vast political and governmental powers which were outside his moral concept of Presidential authority.

Hoover's anti-depression program failed to mold the nation into a cohesive force for recovery. One historian observed that while Hoover could create administrative organization in an emergency, he could not "direct a political party, lead a parliamentary group or organize public opinion." Hoover admitted he was no politician. He regarded politics as theater complete with actors, deceptive greasepaint and contrived dialogue. Without background or interest in political life, Hoover found it difficult to spur legislators and party leaders to action. He experienced equal difficulty in leading the American people. Although a warm, personable man in private, he maintained a colorless, business-directed image to the public whose support he so vitally needed. "[The Presidency] is not a showman's job," he once told an assistant, "I will not step out of character." Faced with the task of rallying national support for recovery, Hoover could not convert his pragmatic program into an aggressive crusade for recovery.

Hoover had been elected President with a Republican majority in Congress, but the midterm election of 1930 wiped out the party's control in the House of Representatives. As the President entered his campaign for a second term in 1932, the reality of a divided Congress and widespread opposition to his policies dampened his whistle-stop appeals for re-election. On November 8, the electorate registered its choice, a decision that had been privately made in the months following "Black Tuesday" in 1929. Hoover's landslide Presidential vote in 1929 turned against him in 1932 to elect Governor Franklin D. Roosevelt of New York to the nation's highest office. In the silence of the voting booth, Hoover's achievements in armament reduction, economic cooperation with Central and South America, child health and conservation were virtually forgotten. His depression recovery program — organization of the Reconstruction Finance Corporation, Home and Farm Loan Banks, the White House economic conferences — was only a faint echo as the voting majority cast its ballot.

In the years following his defeat, the ex-President coldly denounced New Deal policies of government economic intervention and was shunned by the Roosevelt administration as an elder statesman. Hoover remained in the shadows of public life until President Harry S. Truman asked him to coordinate postwar Europe and Asian food relief in 1946 and conduct an economic mission to South America in 1947.

Remaining active throughout his later years, Hoover served as chairman of two committees on reorganization of the Federal government's executive branch under Presidents Truman and Dwight D. Eisenhower. He also published his memoirs in the early 1950s and continued his interest in the Hoover Institution on War, Revolution and Peace at Stanford University which he founded in 1920. After almost 50 years of continual public service, Hoover died in New York City on October 20, 1964, at the age of 90.

Stripped of subjective judgements, Herbert Hoover's achievement in life was a tribute to his concept of individualism in a democracy. His writings and spoken words reveal a firm faith in man's ability to create a more meaningful existence; they provide a challenge to all Americans.
— CHARLES R. FOWLER

Certificates of honorary degrees on the paneled
wall of the Herbert Hoover Library, West Branch, Iowa.

I
THE YEARS OF PREPARATION
1874 - 1914

My boyhood ambition was to be able to earn my own living without the help of anybody, anywhere.

From book, Hoover Off the Record, *by Theodore Joslin, 1934*

But I prefer to think of Iowa as I saw it through the eyes of a ten-year-old boy — and the eyes of all ten-year-old Iowa boys are or should be filled with the wonders of Iowa's streams and woods, of the mystery of growing crops. His days should be filled with adventure and great undertakings, with participation in good and comforting things. I was taken farther West from Iowa when I was ten, to Oregon and thence to that final haven of Iowans — California — where I have clung ever since. Some one may say that these recollections of Iowa are only the illusions of forty years after, but I know better — for I have been back and checked it up. I was told that when I went back everything would have shrunk up and become small and ordinary. For instance, there was Cook's Hill — that great, long hill where, on winter nights, we slid down at terrific speeds with our tummies tight to home-made sleds. I've seen it several times since; it's a good hill and except for the older method of thawing out frozen toes with ice-water the operation needs no modern improvement. The swimming-hole under the willows down by the railroad bridge is still operating efficiently, albeit modern mothers probably compel their youngsters to take a bath to get rid of clean and healthy mud when they come home. The hole still needs to be deepened, however. It is hard to keep from pounding the mud with your hands and feet when you shove off for the thirty feet of a cross-channel swim. And there were the woods down the Burlington track. The denudation of our forests hasn't reached them even yet, and I know there are rabbits still being trapped in cracker-boxes held open by a figure four at the behest of small boys at this very time. I suspect, however, that the conservationists have invented some kind of a closed season before now. One of the bitterest days of my life was in connection with a rabbit. Rabbits fresh from a figure-four trap early on a cold morning are wiggly rabbits, and in the lore of boys of my time it is better to bring them home alive. My brother, being older, had surreptitiously behind the blacksmith shop read in the *Youth's Companion* full directions for rendering live rabbits secure. I say "surreptitiously," for mine was a Quaker family unwilling in those days to have youth corrupted with stronger reading than the Bible, the encyclopedia or those great novels where the hero overcomes the demon rum. Soon after he had acquired this higher learning on rabbits, he proceeded to instruct me to stand still in the cold snow and to hold up the rabbit by its hind feet while with his not over-sharp knife he proposed to puncture two holes between the sinews and back knee joints of the rabbit, through which holes he proposed to tie a string and thus arrive at complete security. Upon the introduction of the operation the resistance of this rabbit was too much for me. I was not only blamed for its escape all the way home and for weeks afterwards, but continuously over the last forty years. I had thought sometimes that I would write the *Youth's Companion* and suggest they make sure that this method is altered. For I never see rabbit tracks across the snowy fields that I do not have a painful recollection of it all.

Nov. 10, 1927, Washington, D.C.
(From book, Hoover After Dinner)

My recollection of my father is of necessity dim indeed. I retain one vivid memento from his time. Playing barefoot around the blacksmith shop, I stepped on a chip of hot iron and carry the brand of Iowa on my foot to this day. Before his death he had parted with the blacksmith shop and had established a comfortable farm implement business. With larger resources and a growing family, he then bought a larger house across the street from the little cottage now preserved by the State of Iowa as my birthplace. The new house was later destroyed but my memories are associated with it.

At the implement shop he had a machine for putting barbs on wire. After the barbs were fixed, the bundles of wire were dipped in hot tar to prevent rust. While no one was looking I undertook an experiment in combustion by putting a lighted stick in the caldron. It produced a smoke

Herbert Hoover was born in this two-room cottage in West Branch, Iowa, on August 10, 1874.

that brought the town running and me speeding the other way in complete terror. Whenever I see a picture of a volcanic eruption I recall that terror. Another experiment in wood carving nearly cut a forefinger off. The scar is still there, but I had compensations among other small boys from my surgical importance.

My recollections of my mother are more vivid and are chiefly of a sweet-faced woman who for two years kept the little family of four together. She took in sewing to add to the family resources. It was only years later that I learned of her careful saving of the $1000 insurance upon my father's life in order that it might help in our education. As a help to her, an uncle, Major Laban Miles, took me to the then Indian Territory for eight or nine months, where I lived with his family. He was United States Indian Agent to the Osage Nation, a position he

held with the affection of the Indians for many years. It was my first train journey and my first long buggy-drive — from Arkansas City to Pawhuska, the agency. Here, with cousins of my own age, I had constant association with the little Indians at the agency school. We learned much aboriginal lore of the woods and streams, and how to make bows and arrows. We attended the Indian Sunday-school which was conducted in English. One Sunday, a visiting missionary, reviewing the service, demanded to know the subject of the day's lesson. At once all the little Indians piped up "Ananias set fire to his wife," this being an etymological impression of "Ananias and Saphira, his wife."

From book, The Memoirs of Herbert Hoover:
The Years of Adventure (1874-1920), *1951*

The long hours of the Quaker meeting required intense restraint on the part of a ten-year-old boy . . .

I am not recommending the good old days, for while the standards of living in food and clothing and shelter were high enough for anybody's health and comfort, there was but little left for the other purposes of living. That is probably one reason why the people of Iowa of that time put more of their time in religious devotion than most of them do now. It certainly did not require as much expenditure as their recreation does today. However, those of you who are acquainted with the Quaker faith, and who know the primitive furnishing of the Quaker meeting-house of those days, the solemnity of the long hours of meeting awaiting the spirit to move some one, will know the intense restraint required in a ten-year-old boy not even to count his toes. All this may not have been recreation, but it was strong training in patience.

Nov. 10, 1927, Washington, D.C.
(From book, Hoover After Dinner)

I was brought here [Newberg, Oregon] 70 years ago to live in the family of my Uncle Dr. Henry John Minthorn, a country doctor.

My first day in Newberg was spent in making acquaintance with lovable Aunt Laura. My Aunt was rather a stern person with disciplinarian ideas. She had few words and they were mostly devoted to moral requirements. But she relaxed at moments when I needed to go fishing or to explore the woods.

When I arrived on the Oregon scene she was busy with my girl cousins making the winter store of pear butter, from pears which grew prolifically in this yard. I had never eaten a pear before as my family circumstances in the Midwest did not permit that exotic luxury. She showed me how to stir the kettle and indicated that I had to keep going without any stops. But at the same time she said, "Thee can eat all the pears thee likes." I liked the idea, and I liked it too much. And then she tucked a sick small boy into bed. I ceased to eat pears — for a while.

One of my chores was to split the wood for stove-size current use. I have had little opinion of split wood as a household fuel ever since. But I can still hear Aunt

Laura calling me from much more desirable occupations, "It is time thee gets in the wood."

My activities hereabouts did not make any great transformation of human society.

81st Birthday Celebration, Newberg, Oregon, Aug. 10, 1955
(From book, Addresses Upon the American Road 1955-1960)

At Salem [Oregon] a blessing came my way in the person of a lady of real understanding — Miss Jennie Gray. Her interest was in boys working in stores and offices. She took me to the small library in the town and borrowed for me a copy of *Ivanhoe*. That opening of the door to a great imaginative world led me promptly through much of Scott and Dickens, often at the cost of sleep. Years later, this reading added to the joys of exploring the towns and countryside in England and Scotland.

From book, The Memoirs of Herbert Hoover:
The Years of Adventure (1874-1920), *1951*

I arrived at Menlo Park — there being no station yet at Palo Alto — with my bicycle, satchel and directions from Professor Swain to go to Adelante Villa, where a Miss Fletcher would furnish me board and tutoring.

Miss Fletcher did her best with charm and patience. No one knew how many students would come to the new University. A certain anxiety that there should be enough no doubt helped me in taking those entrance subjects at which I had failed before. And when the crucial day came I got by with all requirements subject to some "conditions," except that I was one subject short. I earnestly examined the various elective alternatives for a spot where I might attack this final citadel. My association with my doctor uncle stood me in good stead. For by polishing a sound memory and boning all night on two textbooks on physiology, I triumphantly passed in that subject. A Salem boy — Fred Williams — and I moved into Encina Hall, the men's dormitory, the week before

The type of anvil and blacksmith tools used by Herbert Hoover's father, Jesse, who died when his son was only six.

Hoover (right) at 14, with elder brother Theodore ("Tad") Jesse and sister May.

Hoover in 1899, the year he married Lou Henry whom he had met at Stanford University.

I came under the spell of a great scientist and a great teacher...

its opening and were proudly its first inhabitants. Also, the Encina dining room gave so many options in food that I was able to declare my complete independence from mush and milk, which under stiff moral pressure had been my major breakfast course ever since I could remember.

The University opened formally on October 1, 1891. It was a great occasion. Senator and Mrs. Stanford were present. The speeches of Senator Stanford and Dr. David Starr Jordan, the first President, make dry reading today but they were mightily impressive to a youngster. Dr. John Branner, who was to preside over the Department of Geology and Mining, had not yet arrived, so with Professor Swain's guidance I undertook the preparatory subjects that would lead into that department later on. Upon Dr. Branner's arrival I came under the spell of a great scientist and a great teacher, whose friendship lasted over his lifetime.

From book, The Memoirs of Herbert Hoover:
The Years of Adventure (1874-1920), *1951*

rge Fox College, the school in Newberg, Oregon, founded by the
kers, which Hoover attended when it was Pacific Academy.

As an 86-year-old elder statesman, Hoover
spent many informal moments in the library of his
hotel suite in New York City.

George Fox College, the school in Newberg, Oregon, founded by the
Quakers, which Hoover attended when it was Pacific Academy.

Stanford is a coeducational institution, but I had little time to devote to coeds. However, a major event in my life came in my senior year. Miss Lou Henry entered Stanford and the geology laboratories, determined to pursue and teach that subject as a livelihood. As I was Dr. Branner's handy boy in the department, I felt it my duty to aid the young lady in her studies both in the laboratory and in the field. And this call to duty was stimulated by her whimsical mind, her blue eyes, and a broad grinnish smile that came from an Irish ancestor. I was not long in learning that she also was born in Iowa, the same year as myself, and that she was the daughter of a hunting-fishing country banker at Monterey who had no sons and therefore had raised his daughter in the out-of-door life of a boy. After I left college she still had three years to complete her college work. I saw her once or twice during this period. We carried on a correspondence.

From book, The Memoirs of Herbert Hoover:
The Years of Adventure (1874-1920), *1951*

We endowed our university with a football team. Probably because I had been able to save the money for uniforms and equipment of the baseball team, I was made the manager. We arranged a game with the University of California to be played on the University's second Thanksgiving Day. The game was to take place at the Haight Street baseball grounds in San Francisco. We had seats for a total of 15,000 fans. We bought new uniforms for our teams from a dealer on the sales expectations. We printed seat-numbered tickets for only 10,000 as we did not expect more visitors than that number. When the game came on, two things happened to disturb the managers.

First, the attendance piled up to nearly 20,000. We had no such supply of tickets. So we set up an alley of our college boys from the box offices to the gates and sold tickets for cash — the purchasers being carefully watched so that no outsiders crowded in without having first paid their respects to the box office. At that time few bills were in use in California. We dealt in silver and gold.

19

At 23 Hoover was in sparsely populated Western Australia successfully managing a gold mine.

Berton W. Crandall Photograph Collection

grain bags, and sat up most of the night counting it. I had never seen $30,000 before. The bank the next morning found that we had $18 more. We were well financed for the next season.

From book, The Memoirs of Herbert Hoover:
The Years of Adventure (1874-1920), *1951*

Somewhat later in the siege* Mrs. Hoover and I and our engineering staff returned to our own house for a base, as it had not been hit. Late one evening, however, a shell banged through a back window and then, exploding, blew out the front door and surroundings. Mrs. Hoover, after a long day at the hospital, was sitting in a side room playing solitaire. She never stopped the game. A few evenings later several shells came close and finally one exploded in the compound across the street where the Chinese were living. Agnew and I rushed over and found that it had landed in Tong Shao-yi's place, killing his wife and baby and slightly injuring one of his children. Tong was naturally distracted, but helped us to gather up the other children. Agnew, Tong and I, each carrying one and leading others, brought them across to our house. . . .

From book, The Memoirs of Herbert Hoover:
The Years of Adventure (1874-1920), *1951*

The impression I have held of the Chinese people is one of abiding admiration. Ninety per cent of the huge mass live so close to the starvation line that someone falls below it in nearly every village every year. Yet they live with patience, with tolerance. They have the deepest fidelity to family ties, and the fullest affection for their children. They work harder and more hours than any other race in the world. True, they are superstitious beyond belief, but they have a vivid sense of humor. They are courageous, as witness the armies they have created.

From book, The Memoirs of Herbert Hoover:
The Years of Adventure (1874-1920), *1951*

Pre-war England was the most comfortable place in which to live in the whole world. That is, if one had the means to take part in its upper life. The servants were the best trained and the most loyal of any nationality. The machinery for joy and for keeping busy doing nothing was the most perfect in the world. The countryside was of unending beauty, and above all, to Americans, its

The cash piled up behind our entrance selling boys to the extent it spilled on the floors; we had to rent a washboiler and a dishpan from nearby householders for the price of a free ticket.

And while these difficulties were being solved, the captains of the two teams turned up, demanding to know where was the football. We had overlooked that detail and had to delay the game for a half-hour while we sent downtown for two pigskins.

I did not see the game, but to our astonishment we won. After the game the California manager and I retired to a hotel with our money, now transferred to

---

* During the summer of 1900 the foreign settlement in Tientsin, China, underwent a siege from the Chinese for about a month.

great background of our common history, literature and institutions was of constant inspiration. To London came the greatest music, the greatest drama, the greatest art, and the best food in the world. The polite living in city and country breathed hospitality itself. Over our years of sojourning, we became greatly attached to our house on Campden Hill and to the stream of American and British friends with whom we came in contact. We spent many happy times there. . . .

From book, The Memoirs of Herbert Hoover: The Years of Adventure (1874-1920), *1951*

I can, perhaps, without over-sentimentality, give a note I wrote to Mrs. Hoover in 1938, when I revisited England after having been away nearly twenty years:

While in London I sneaked away on a visit of unalloyed sentiment. I stole out of the hotel alone, found a cab, told the driver the old formula — "Kensington, High Street, Horton Street to the Red House." On the way, my mind traveled over the thousands of times we had driven along Pall Mall, Knightsbridge and High Street, nearly every house of which was still unchanged. We came to High Street, and as always, I had to direct the cabby to take the second turning to the left beyond the church. And the church was the same as when the boys used to attend all weddings as doorstep-observers, returning to tell us if the red carpet or the awning were up — that service being five shillings extra — and how many bridesmaids or how many peals of the bells there were — those being two shillings sixpence each.

I came to the door of the Red House, flooded with memories of the months we had lived there, alternatively with our New York and California homes for nearly twenty years. How we had first come, as a couple, from stays in Australia or China or Russia or Burma, or New York or the Continent; then when we had brought the babies; then when I would return from long journeys to meet you all again.

At the door, even after twenty years, I automatically fumbled in my pocket for the key. I rang the bell, gave the very stiff butler my card, and asked if I might see the lady of the house, explaining that I was an American who had lived in this house many years ago, was in London only for a few days, and would like to walk through the rooms and the garden again. The butler seemed nonplussed, but came back after some minutes, and through the partially opened door, announced, "Her Ladyship is not in." I was prepared for this British event with a ten-shilling note, sufficiently exposed, and suggested that perhaps he would let me see any part of the house that was not in use at the moment. To the left was the oak-panelled library with its fine

In 1902 Hoover was a junior partner in a large mining firm with headquarters in London.

England before the First World War was the most comfortable place to live . . .

She is part of passing England . . .

fireplace and its leaded glass bookcases — the same as ever. I imagined again, sitting on the opposite side of the desk from you, with the manuscripts and reference books of Agricola, piled between us, as we worked over the translation of *De Re Metallica*. Again I saw "Pete" at the little table in the corner, making marks and announcing that he was writing a book too; and "Bub" clambering into his mother's lap and demanding to know what the book said. The dining room was the same walnut-panelled room and evoked all kinds of memories of the multitude of happy gatherings which had filled it. The living room had been redecorated from its old neutral tints to modern white French and was a repellent stranger. The century-old mulberry tree, which we had nursed for years with steel I beams and which had given character to the garden, was gone and replaced by some formal bushes.

Altogether my mind was a maze of revived emotional pictures and some disappointments. But by now the butler was standing on one foot and filled with anxieties — and to finish him, I shook his hand, which I suppose no "gentleman" had ever done before.

Your old parlor-maid, grim-faced Lovell, came to Claridges [hotel]. She timidly inquired of Perrin if she might see me. She asked me to thank "Madame" for sending her a nice card every Christmas and especially for the 'elp you have given her from the White 'ouse in the unemployment times and to inquire after the 'ealth of the "Young Masters" — and her stolid old face softened at every reference to the "Young Masters." I suspect, in her memory, they were still little more than babies. I thought perhaps she came for more 'elp and not wanting to offend her I remarked that if she got in a tight place again she should write to the "Madame." She replied at once, "Oh, no, I 'ave a 'nice place' with a family in 'yde Park, but they are not the likes of 'Madame.' Besides, when I sent the money back to 'Madame' she would not take it and told me to put it in the bank in case 'ard times come again and I 'ave it."

So you will see she has never recovered an "h" and I have discovered your secret transactions. I directed one of the boys to take her down to the afternoon tea then going on in the hotel with the fashionables of London and to treat her like the real lady she is in her heart. He reported that her major observation was "These waiters is not trained to serve tea properly." She is a part of passing England.

From book, The Memoirs of Herbert Hoover:
The Years of Adventure (1874-1920), *1951*

At my ship's table sat an English lady of great cultivation and a happy mind, who contributed much to the evanescent conversation on government, national customs, literature, art, industry, and whatnot. We were coming up New York harbor at the final farewell breakfast, when she turned to me and said:

"I hope you will forgive my dreadful curiosity, but I should like awfully to know — what is your profession?"

I replied that I was an engineer. She emitted an involuntary exclamation, and "Why, I thought you were a gentleman!"

From book, The Memoirs of Herbert Hoover:
The Years of Adventure (1874-1920), *1951*

The happiest period of all humanity in the Western World in ten centuries was the twenty-five years before the First World War. It was the habit of intellectuals to disparage those times as callous, crude, dominated by bad taste and greed, with privilege to the few and poverty and squalor to the many. We have seen a continuous "debunking" of the good by the concentration upon the secondary evils.

Yet in the eyes of a professional observer, this period stands in high contrast to the quarter century that had gone before.

The world had experienced half a century of freedom from great wars. The long peace had buried the fear of war. The world believed that war, except perhaps for a sporadic outburst now and then, among the Balkans, was a thing of the past. The Four Horsemen seemed only an ancient Biblical story. . . .

But with a single spark the evil spirits rose to strangle all reason. The world in a storm of emotion gave way to fear, hate and destruction.

Although I was more than ordinarily familiar with eastern European national movements, I was not one of those subsequent know-it-all citizens who saw war coming. There was not one out of a million so little confident of the future as to believe it possible.

On June 28, 1914, when news came of the assassination of the Archduke at Sarajevo, the world took it as just another of those habitual Balkan lapses into barbarism — and we went about our accustomed business with little more thought than that.

From book, The Memoirs of Herbert Hoover:
The Years of Adventure (1874-1920), *1951*

This nineteenth century landscape, "Dedham Vale with Ploughmen",
by John Constable, is typical of the English countryside enjoyed by Hoover and his family
during their many years in Britain in the early 1900's.

II
THE GREAT WAR AND ITS AFTERMATH
1915 - 1919

It is difficult to portray the immensity of the tasks in great famines. Statistics throw but a dim light on the scene of organization. But perhaps the reader will have a better understanding of these tasks if I relate that during the period the United States was in the First World War — from April, 1917, to the Armistice, in November, 1918 — we provided the necessary margins of food, medicine, and clothing to ten nations of about 157,000,000 people. After the Armistice, we had to organize thirty-two nations with 400,000,000 people, of whom about 220,000,000 were in acute famine. And after the Second World War, to meet the world-wide famine, we had need to organize fifty nations of over 1,500,000,000 people, of whom 800,000,000, without overseas supplies, would have had less food than the prisoners in Buchenwald. Most of these 800,000,000 would have died of mass starvation or its mercy, disease.

From book, An American Epic, *by Herbert Hoover, 1959*

Since the sufferings of the early Pilgrim fathers, the American people have never known famine. Even in the Confederate States during the Civil War there was enough food to maintain public health.

No one who has not seen famine with his own eyes can have understanding of its hideous reality. Mothers at every meal watch the wilting away of their children. Gaunt mothers search for scraps of food, carry emaciated children too feeble to walk. Long streams of refugees flee from the famine areas, carrying their children and a few possessions, with many dead lying at the roadsides. Few people die directly from starvation, for disease intervenes. The hospitals and children's refuges are crowded with all who can lie on the floors. The dead lie unburied in heaps. And even worse things happen which I do not repeat here.

From book, An American Epic, *by Herbert Hoover, 1959*

At four o'clock on the morning of May 7 I was awakened by a troubled servant, who explained that there was a messenger waiting with an important document which he would put into no hands other than mine. It was the printed draft of the Treaty [of Versailles], which was to be handed to the Germans that day. At once I scanned its important parts. Although I had known the gist of many of the segments, I had not before had opportunity to envision it as a whole. Aside from the League Covenant, many provisions had been settled without considering their effect on others.

I certainly had no admiration for the conduct of the German militarists. But if the world was to have peace, it had, in my mind, to choose one of two alternatives: to reduce Germany to such poverty and political degradation that initiative and genius would be extinguished; or to give her terms that would permit the new representative government under President Ebert to live with the hope that free government might develop the nation as a peaceful member of the family of mankind. If this were not done, there would come either a return of the sullen militarists or the already infectious Communists — both with aggression in their souls.

I was convinced that the terms set up in this draft of the Treaty would degrade all Europe and that peace for the long run could not be built on these foundations. I believed the Treaty contained the seeds of another war. It seemed to me that the economic provisions alone would pull down the whole Continent and, in the end, injure the United States.

I arose at early daylight and went for a walk in the deserted streets. Within a few blocks I met General Smuts and John Maynard Keynes of the British Delegation. We seemed to have come together by some sort of telepathy. It flashed into all our minds why each was walking about at that time of morning. Each was greatly disturbed. We agreed that the consequences of many parts of the proposed Treaty would ultimately bring destruction. We also agreed that we would do what we could among our own nationals to point out the dangers.

General Smuts had full knowledge of Old World diplomacy, an independent mind and often real statesmanship. Keynes was the economist for the British Delegation.

A food relief poster from the
1917-1919 period when Hoover served as
United States Food Administrator.

FOOD WILL WIN THE WAR

You came here seeking Freedom
You must now help to preserve it

WHEAT is needed for the allies
Waste nothing

UNITED STATES FOOD ADMINISTRATION

Lloyd George apparently did not like him and referred to him as the "Puck of Economics." He had a brilliant mind, powerful in analysis, and the gift of expression. Like most intellectuals, he was usually groping for new shapes and forms for the world, rather than for wisdom in what to do next. That sort of mind has a high place in the world, although it sometimes gets on the nerves of the fellow who must keep the machinery of organization operating in the meantime. However, Keynes and I agreed fully on the economic consequences of the Treaty.

From book, The Ordeal of Woodrow Wilson, *by Herbert Hoover, 1958*

I called on Premier Clemenceau [of France] on September 3 to express my appreciation for his undeviating support of my work. In another memoir, I have recalled:

... He was in a gloomy mood, saying, "There will be another world war in your time and you will be needed back in Europe."

From book, The Ordeal of Woodrow Wilson, *by Herbert Hoover, 1958*

For a moment at the time of the Armistice, Mr. Wilson rose to intellectual domination of most of the civilized world. With his courage and eloquence, he carried a message of hope for the independence of nations, the freedom of men and lasting peace. Never since his time has any man risen to the political and spiritual heights that came to him. His proclaimed principles of self-government and independence aided the spread of freedom to twenty-two races at the time of the Armistice.

But he was to find that his was a struggle between the concepts of the New and Old Worlds. European statesmen were dominated by the forces of hate and revenge of their peoples for grievous wrongs; by the economic prostration of their peoples; and by the ancient system of imperial spoils. Mr. Wilson was forced to compromise with their demands in order to save the League, confident that it would in time right the wrongs that had been done.

One of his colleagues at Paris, General Jan Smuts, said of him:

At a time of the deepest darkness and despair he had raised aloft a light to which all eyes had turned. He had spoken divine words of healing and consolation to a broken humanity. His lofty moral idealism seemed for a moment to dominate the brutal passions which had torn the Old World asunder....

... Without hesitation he plunged into that inferno of human passions.... There were six months of agonized waiting, during which the world situation rapidly deteriorated. And then he emerged with the Peace Treaty. It was not a Wilson peace.... This was a Punic peace....

... The Paris peace lost an opportunity as unique as the great war itself. In destroying the moral idealism born of the sacrifices of the war it did almost as much as the war itself in shattering the structure of Western civilization.

... It was not Wilson who failed.... It was the human spirit itself that failed at Paris....

From book, The Ordeal of Woodrow Wilson, *by Herbert Hoover, 1958*

With [Woodrow Wilson's] death ended a Greek tragedy, not on the stage of imagination, but in the lives of nations. And as in the tragedies of old the inspiring words and deeds of men who failed still live.

From book, The Ordeal of Woodrow Wilson, *by Herbert Hoover, 1958*

No purpose can be served by reciting the events of the following fifteen years, but the Treaty [of Versailles] certainly sowed the dragon's teeth of future revolutions and trouble. The reparations and controls stifled German recovery and ultimately her collapse dragged the world into economic depression. The insistence upon weakening Germany by separating large segments of the German race will yet bring explosions to the world.

The New World imported notion of racial boundaries and independence of states based upon race, and the denial of such settlements for economic or other reasons to Germans and other minorities increased fires of resistance and discontent. And the New World theory of whole disarmament was applied only to disarming the enemy and simply implanted again the seeds of war. The New World cry of justice and right became a touchstone upon which a thousand injustices incurable by treaties were proved and in proving lighted the flames of war. I could pursue the subject at great length. The fact is that if the Allies had made their own kind of peace — no doubt a peace based upon balances of power and force and old diplomacy — it would have been a more durable peace than the mixture. Still better, infinitely better, would have been the peace Woodrow Wilson brought to Europe.

More importantly the subsequent conduct of the dominant Powers contributed greatly to destroy the growth of democracy in the old enemy areas. The words of many British and French statesmen could be cited to show that this is understatement. There are a hundred incidents to prove it. For instance, in the spring of 1932 I received appeals from the democratic leaders of Ger-

The inspiring words and deeds of
men who failed still live . . .

many to aid them in securing moderation of certain parts of the Treaty of Versailles which were endangering the survival of the Republic. At that time they were being pressed by the Communists on one side and the Nazis on the other. The dangers were real and great. The changes they desired in no way endangered any other nation. But the response of the French Prime Minister to my urging through Ambassador Gibson during the Disarmament Conference at Geneva was: "I will not consent to changing one atom of the Treaty of Versailles."

From book, America's First Crusade, *by Herbert Hoover, 1941*

In September, 1919, Mrs. Hoover, Allan, and I boarded the *Aquitania* en route home. I was sure of two things: I wanted relief from European duty. I understood fully why our ancestors had moved away from it.

After five years concerned with the World War, we looked only in one direction — to get home to the West. I had not been in California for nearly six years. Our family had been together for only a few scattered and fitful months. I saw them only at meals. And always at these meals, even sometimes including breakfast, we had for guests men with whom I was working. But now we promised ourselves we would take the first train for the West, get out the fishing rods, motor into the mountains, and live again.

This program sustained a jolt when word came to the steamer that the engineers of America were going to give me a great reception and a public dinner in New York. And they demanded a speech. Speeches were not a part

of my treasured occasions of life, and the preparation of "some remarks" cast a gloom over the rest of the voyage. The speech turned out to be only a sort of review of what we had done and the forces of social disruption still current in the world.

With the reception and speech over, we went West — hoping that I had served my turn in public life and might now devote myself to a reasonable existence. And, of more importance, I hoped to renew association with a great lady and two highly satisfactory boys.

I was not quite forty-five years of age and was confident I had time to reestablish myself in my profession,

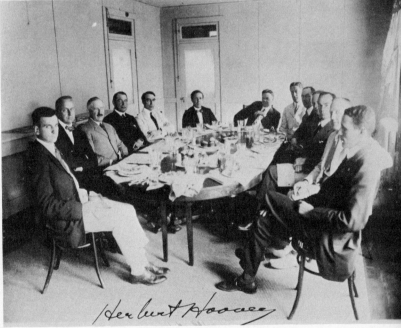

Above: A photograph taken during
World War I shows Hoover (end of table, arm raised)
during an informal luncheon with United States
Food Administration staff members.
Left: Hoover (seated, center)
with members of the Commission for the
Relief of Belgium.

Berton W. Crandall Photograph Collection

Berton W. Crandall Photograph Collection

Many flour sacks that carried
American relief commission food to Belgium
during World War I were returned by grateful recipients
with handsewn appreciation messages.

Posters created for the U.S.
Food Administration were graphic appeals
for food conservation. A Hoover
life-saving station was a household
which supported the food-saving program.

even though all my clients had scattered to the four winds. I opened offices in San Francisco and New York and hinted that I would undertake engineering work again. We resumed housekeeping in our cottage on the Stanford campus. Mrs. Hoover, the boys and I went camping, motoring, and fishing in the mountains just as we had so often dreamed and planned.

However, soon after the return to California, I made discoveries which disturbed my ideas of blissful living. I had come out of the seething social and political movements and economic chaos of Europe. I quickly found that America was not a quiet pool either. The country was in the midst of the inevitable after-war economic headache. Troubles rising from war demobilization brought general unrest and need for many readjustments. And the natural slump from the high wartime level of altruism and idealism complicated all Americans' thinking. We were also faced with gigantic tasks of physical reconstruction from the war. I had expected that.

In addition, the bitter conflict over the Treaty and the League of Nations cut across all issues.

Another disturbance was a personal matter. Hundreds of letters a day followed me about. Cables, telegrams, and telephone calls tracked me down in the forests and on the streams. Every day the press demanded statements on something or other. The magazines asked for articles, and, above all, it seemed to me that the American appetite for speeches had been unduly expanded by war exercises of that art. Every national gathering and every lunch club wanted speeches. Leaders of national movements bombarded me with requests to lend my name to their lists of sponsors.

With a desire for a little respite, I stated in answer to this clamor and demands from the press, as to what I was going to do:

I plan to adhere to the following rules for one month:

I will reply to no telephone calls, I am spending a month with two vigorous small boys. I do not want to be tied to the end of a telephone all day.

I do not myself read any communication which exceeds more than one page. These rules are solely for my own good.

I must decline the honor of speaking at sixty-four public meetings to which I have received invitations. I am satisfied that the American people will be gratified to find a citizen who wants to keep still. This rule is for the public good.

All this is subject to the reservation that nothing turns up to irritate my conscience or peace of mind.

I offer this intimate disclosure of private affairs so that it may be seen that I contemplate no mischief against this Commonwealth.

From book, The Memoirs of Herbert Hoover:
The Cabinet and the Presidency (1920-1933), *1951, 1952*

A statue of Isis, the ancient Egyptian goddess of the harvest, was a post-World War I gift from Belgian school children. It now stands in Hoover Park, West Branch, Iowa.

III

THE YEARS OF PEACE
AND RECONSTRUCTION

1920 - 1927

Much of our discontent takes the form of resentment against the inequalities in the distribution of the sacrifices of war. Both silently and vocally there is complaint that while some died, others ran no risk, and yet others profited. For these complaints there is adequate justification. The facts are patent. However, no conceivable human intelligence would be able to manage the conduct of war so as to see that all sacrifices and burdens should be distributed equitably. War is destruction, and we should blame war for its injustices, not a social system whose object is construction. The submergence of the individual, however, in the struggle of the race could be but temporary — its continuance through the crushing of individual action and its inequities would, if for no other reason, destroy the foundations of our civilization.

From book, American Individualism, *by Herbert Hoover, 1922*

... It is not the individualism of other countries for which I would speak, but the individualism of America. Our individualism differs from all others because it embraces these great ideals: that while we build our society upon the attainment of the individual, we shall safeguard to every individual an equality of opportunity to take that position in the community to which his intelligence, character, ability, and ambition entitle him; that we keep the social solution free from frozen strata of classes; that we shall stimulate effort of each individual to achievement; that through an enlarging sense of responsibility and understanding we shall assist him to this attainment; while he in turn must stand up to the emery wheel of competition.

From book, American Individualism, *by Herbert Hoover, 1922*

Salvation will not come to us out of the wreckage of individualism. What we need today is steady devotion to a better, brighter, broader individualism — an individualism that carries increasing responsibility and service to our fellows. Our need is not for a way out but for a way forward.

From book, American Individualism, *by Herbert Hoover, 1922*

Individualism cannot be maintained as the foundation of a society if it looks to only legalistic justice based upon contracts, property, and political equality. Such legalistic safeguards are themselves not enough. In our individualism we have long since abandoned the *laissez faire* of the eighteenth century — the notion that it is "every man for himself and the devil take the hindmost." We abandoned that when we adopted the ideal of equality of opportunity — the fair chance of Abraham Lincoln. We have confirmed its abandonment in terms of legislation, of social and economic justice — in part because we have learned that social injustice is the destruction of justice itself. We have learned that the impulse to production can only be maintained at a high pitch if there is a fair division of the product. We have also learned that fair division can only be obtained by certain restrictions on the strong and the dominant.

From book, American Individualism, *by Herbert Hoover, 1922*

But those are utterly wrong who say that individualism has as its only end the acquisition and preservation of private property — the selfish snatching and hoarding of the common product. Our American individualism, indeed, is only in part an economic creed. It aims to provide opportunity for self-expression, not merely economically, but spiritually as well. Private property is not a fetich in America. The crushing of the liquor trade without a cent of compensation, with scarcely even a discussion of it, does not bear out the notion that we give property rights any headway over human rights. ...

From book, American Individualism, *by Herbert Hoover, 1922*

To curb the forces in business which would destroy equality of opportunity and yet to maintain the initiative and creative faculties of our people are the twin objects we must attain. To preserve the former we must regulate that type of activity that would dominate: To preserve the latter, the Government must keep out of production and distribution of commodities and services. This is the deadline between our system and socialism. Regulation to prevent domination and unfair practices,

A bust of Herbert Hoover in the Hoover Institution for War, Revolution and Peace at Stanford University, California.

Leadership is
a quality of the
individual . . .

yet preserving rightful initiative, are in keeping with our social foundations. Nationalization of industry or business is their negation.

From book, American Individualism, *by Herbert Hoover, 1922*

Leadership is a quality of the individual. It is the individual alone who can function in the world of intellect and in the field of leadership. If democracy is to secure its authorities in morals, religion, and statesmanship, it must stimulate leadership from its own mass. Human leadership cannot be replenished by selection like queen bees, by divine right or bureaucracies, but by the free rise of ability, character, and intelligence.

From book, American Individualism, *by Herbert Hoover, 1922*

We in America have had too much experience of life to fool ourselves into pretending that all men are equal in ability, in character, in intelligence, in ambition. That was part of the clap-trap of the French Revolution. We have grown to understand that all we can hope to assure to the individual through government is liberty, justice, intellectual welfare, equality of opportunity, and stimulation to service. . . .

From book, American Individualism, *by Herbert Hoover, 1922*

On the philosophic side we can agree at once that intelligence, character, courage, and the divine spark of the human soul are alone the property of individuals. These do not lie in agreements, in organizations, in institutions, in masses, or in groups. They abide alone in the individual mind and heart.

From book, American Individualism, *by Herbert Hoover, 1922*

My period of popularity lasted nearly fourteen years [1919-1932], which seems about the average. When the ultimate bump came, I was well fortified to

An Iowa village in the region of Hoover's boyhood. He had a lifelong admiration
for the qualities of citizens in America's small towns.

Hoover lived in this house in Washington, D. C., when he served as Secretary of Commerce from 1921 to 1928.

accept it philosophically and, in fact, to welcome it, for democracy is a harsh employer.

In the ensuing period, also of fourteen years, I succeeded in reaching fairly deep unpopularity in consequence of the depression, fighting the New Deal, opposing World War II and its subsequent political policies. But after this second term of fourteen years some people began to think I had been right, and life was more complimentary.

From book, The Memoirs of Herbert Hoover:
The Cabinet and the Presidency (1920-1933), *1951, 1952*

President Harding died in August, 1923, after two and one-half years in office. He was a kind of dual personality. The responsibilities of the White House gave him a real spiritual lift. He deeply wanted to make a name as President. He had real quality in geniality, in good will and in ability for pleasing address. He was not a man with either the experience or the intellectual quality that the position needed. But he was neither a "reactionary" nor a "radical." For instance, I relate later on

how he opposed the leading bankers by demanding supervision of their foreign loans. Likewise he stood up against the whole steel industry when he backed the abolition of the twelve-hour day and the seven-day week. He vetoed the so-called McNary-Haugen bill, which provided a regimentation of farmers.

On one occasion Attorney General Daugherty had got out an injunction against railway employees then on strike. The morning papers brought me the news. I was outraged by its obvious transgression of the most rudimentary rights of the men. Walking over to the Cabinet meeting that morning, I met Secretary [of State Charles Evans] Hughes. He said that it was outrageous in law as well as morals. I suggested that he raise the question in Cabinet. He replied that it scarcely came within his function as Secretary of State to challenge the actions of the Attorney General, and suggested that as Secretary of Commerce, interested in the economic consequences, I had the right to do this. He stated he would support me if I spoke out. When the Cabinet convened, I expressed myself fully and called on Hughes to verify the legal points of my protest. He did it vigorously. Daugherty

Democracy is a harsh employer . . .

was obviously flabbergasted, and when Harding turned upon him demanding explanation of this illegal action could only mumble that the objectionable passages were approved by the lawyers as being within the constitutional rights of the government. Harding very abruptly instructed him to withdraw those sections of the injunction at once. Daugherty dropped the whole action as quickly as possible.

Harding encouraged me in everything I wanted to do. I never knew him to give a promise that he did not keep. Nor did he ever ask me to make an appointment to office except in one minor instance.

From book, The Memoirs of Herbert Hoover:
The Cabinet and the Presidency (1920-1933), *1951, 1952*

Before Mr. Coolidge came to the Presidency, I had only a secondary acquaintance with him — such as one gets by dinner contacts. He was reputed to be a most taciturn man. This was true in his relations with the general run of people and with the press. With his associates there was little of taciturnity. Many times over the five years he sent for men to come to the White House after dinner just to talk an hour or two. He had a fund of New England stories and a fine, dry wit. After my election in 1928, he undertook to give me some fatherly advice as to how to run the White House. He said: "You have to stand every day three or four hours of visitors. Nine-tenths of them want something they ought not to have. If you keep dead-still they will run down in three or four minutes. If you even cough or smile they will start up all over again."

Mr. Coolidge was well equipped by education, experience, and moral courage for the Presidency. He was the incarnation of New England horse sense and was endowed with certain Puritan rigidities that served the nation well. He possessed New England thrift to the ultimate degree, and his tight hold on government expenditures and his constant reduction of public debt were its fine expression.

He was most reluctant to take any action in advance of the actual explosion of trouble. One of his sayings was, "If you see ten troubles coming down the road, you can be sure that nine will run into the ditch before they reach you and you have to battle with only one of them." It was a philosophy that served well while the nation was making a rapid convalescence from its war wounds. The

trouble with this philosophy was that when the tenth trouble reached him he was wholly unprepared, and it had by that time acquired such momentum that it spelled disaster. The outstanding instance was the rising boom and orgy of mad speculation which began in 1927, in respect to which he rejected or sidestepped all our anxious urgings and warnings to take action. The country was prosperous and I suspect that he enjoyed the phrase "Coolidge prosperity" more than any other tag which the newspapers and the public pinned on him.

Mr. Coolidge was a real conservative, probably the equal of Benjamin Harrison. He quickly dissolved our controls over foreign loans. He was a fundamentalist in religion, in the economic and social order, and in fishing. On one of his summer vacations, when he started in that art to which he was a stranger, he fished with worms to the horror of all fly fishermen.

From book, The Memoirs of Herbert Hoover:
The Cabinet and the Presidency (1920-1933), *1951, 1952*

The western radio had been engaged for a half-hour for me to make a supposedly important speech in the Mountain states. The chairman, who had never had such an opportunity to address the whole West before, used a large part of the radio time. During his ecstasy, the others on the platform pulled his coattail repeatedly. Finally he launched out a backward, random mule kick which reached the shinbones of the lady chairman, who sat immediately behind him. She did not applaud.

From book, The Memoirs of Herbert Hoover:
The Cabinet and the Presidency (1920-1933), *1951, 1952*

I received a lasting impression from [the 1927 Mississippi flood experience]. I had organized relief among many peoples in Europe. One of our difficulties there had been to find sufficient intelligence, organizational ability and leadership in the many villages and towns to carry on the local work. But in this organization among Americans the merest suggestion sparked efficient and devoted organization — indeed often in advance of specific request. The reasons for this reach to the very base of our American system of life. In this there also lies a special tribute to the peoples of these States.

From book, The Memoirs of Herbert Hoover:
The Cabinet and the Presidency (1920-1933), *1951, 1952*

IV
THE PRESIDENCY
1928 - 1932

Our purpose is to build in this nation a human society, not an economic system. We wish to increase the efficiency and productivity of our country, but its final purpose is happier homes. We shall succeed through the faith, the loyalty, the self-sacrifice, the devotion to eternal ideals which live today in every American.

Acceptance of Nomination, Stanford University Stadium, Palo Alto, California, Aug. 11, 1928 (from book, The New Day)

Our problems of the past seven years have been problems of reconstruction; our problems of the future are problems of construction. They are problems of progress.

Acceptance of Nomination, Stanford University Stadium, Palo Alto, California, Aug. 11, 1928 (from book, The New Day)

The Presidency is more than an administrative office. It must be the symbol of American ideals. The high and the lowly must be seen with the same eyes, met in the same spirit. It must be the instrument by which national conscience is livened and it must under the guidance of the Almighty interpret and follow that conscience.

Campaign Speech, West Branch, Iowa, Aug. 21, 1928 (from book, The New Day)

American labor has been the first labor body in the world that has had the intelligence and courage to realize and express the fact that increased wages and salaries must in the long run be based upon a sharing of labor in the savings made through industrial and commercial efficiency. Within the past few months British labor has followed this lead of American labor. That is, if we are able by labor-saving machinery and reduction of the wastes in industry to decrease the cost of production of an article, we know by long experience that a train of consequences of the highest importance follow. Wages in that industry will rise, prices decrease, consumption increase at home and in our foreign markets, the demand for labor is enlarged, and

our standards of living improve. The ancient bitter opposition to improved methods on the ancient theory that it more than temporarily deprives men of employment, which is still maintained in some parts of the world, has no place in the gospel of American progress.

Campaign Speech, Newark, New Jersey, Sept. 17, 1928 (from book, The New Day)

To me the foundation of American life rests upon the home and the family. I read into these great economic forces, these intricate and delicate relations of the government with business and with our political and social life, but one supreme end — that we reinforce the ties that bind together the millions of our families, that we strengthen the security, the happiness, and the independence of every home.

My conception of America is a land where men and women may walk in ordered freedom in the independent conduct of their occupations; where they may enjoy the advantages of wealth, not concentrated in the hands of the few but spread through the lives of all; where they build and safeguard their homes, and give to their children the fullest advantages and opportunities of American life; where every man shall be respected in the faith that his conscience and his heart direct him to follow; where a contented and happy people, secure in their liberties, free from poverty and fear, shall have the leisure and impulse to seek a fuller life.

Some may ask where all this may lead beyond mere material progress. It leads to a release of the energies of men and women from the dull drudgery of life to a wider vision and a higher hope. It leads to the opportunity for greater and greater service, not alone from man to man in our own land, but from our country to the whole world. It leads to an America, healthy in body, healthy in spirit, unfettered, youthful, eager — with a vision searching beyond the farthest horizons, with an open mind, sympathetic and generous.

Campaign Speech, New York, New York, Oct. 22, 1928 (from book, The New Day)

It is a false liberalism that interprets itself into the government operation of commercial business. Every step of bureaucratizing of the business of our country poisons the very roots of liberalism — that is, political equality, free speech, free assembly, free press,

Accepting the Republican nomination for
President in 1932, Hoover addressed an audience at
Constitution Hall, Washington, D. C.

Hoover, as President, greeted a crowd in Pennsylvania
during his 1932 campaign for re-election.

and equality of opportunity. It is the road not to more liberty, but to less liberty. Liberalism should be found not striving to spread bureaucracy but striving to set bounds to it. True liberalism seeks all legitimate freedom first in the confident belief that without such freedom the pursuit of all other blessings and benefits is vain. That belief is the foundation of all American progress, political as well as economic.

Campaign Speech, New York, New York, Oct. 22, 1928
(from book, The New Day)

The worst plague in the campaign was the religious issue. Governor Smith was the first Presidential candidate of Catholic faith, and for that matter I was the first Quaker. Religion is a difficult matter to handle politically. Even to mention religious questions was enough to fan the flames of bigotry. I tried to stamp out the issue in my acceptance speech on August 11, 1928, by a forthright reference:

In this land, dedicated to tolerance, we still find outbreaks of intolerance. I come of Quaker stock. My ancestors were persecuted for their beliefs. Here they sought and found religious freedom. By blood and conviction I stand for religious tolerance both in act and in spirit. The glory of our American ideals is the right of every man to worship God according to the dictates of his own conscience.

From book, The Memoirs of Herbert Hoover:
The Cabinet and the Presidency (1920-1933), *1951, 1952*

Governor Alfred E. Smith, the Democratic candidate, was a natural born gentleman. Both of us had come up from the grass roots or the pavements, and from boyhood had learned the elements of sportsmanship. During the campaign he said no word and engaged in no action that did not comport with the highest levels. I paid a natural tribute to him when speaking in New York during the campaign, and he did so to me when speaking in California. In after years, when I was often associated with him in public matters, we mutually agreed that we had one deep satisfaction from the battle. No word had been spoken or misrepresentation made by either of us which prevented sincere friendship the day after election.

From book, The Memoirs of Herbert Hoover:
The Cabinet and the Presidency (1920-1933), *1951, 1952*

...All this majestic advance should not obscure the constant dangers from which self-government must be safeguarded. The strong man must at all times be alert to the attack of insidious disease.

The most malign of all these dangers today is disregard and disobedience of law. Crime is increasing. Confidence in rigid and speedy justice is decreasing. I am not prepared to believe that this indicates any decay in the moral fiber of the American people. I am not prepared to believe that it indicates an impotence of the Federal Government to enforce its laws.

It is only in part due to the additional burdens imposed upon our judicial system by the eighteenth amendment [prohibition]. The problem is much wider than that. Many influences had increasingly complicated and weakened our law enforcement organization long before the adoption of the eighteenth amendment....

Reform, reorganization and strengthening of our whole judicial and enforcement system both in civil and criminal sides have been advocated for years by statesmen, judges, and bar associations. First steps toward that end should not longer be delayed. Rigid and expeditious justice is the first safeguard of freedom, the basis of all ordered liberty, the vital force of progress. It must not come to be in our Republic that it can be defeated by the indifference of the citizen, by exploitation of the delays and entanglements of the law, or by combinations of criminals. Justice must not fail because the agencies of enforcement are either delinquent or inefficiently organized. To consider these evils, to find their remedy, is the most sore necessity of our times....

The election has again confirmed the determination of the American people that regulation of private enterprise and not Government ownership or operation is the course rightly to be pursued in our relation to business. In recent years we have established a differentiation in the whole method of business regulation between the industries which produce and distribute commodities on the one hand and public utilities on the other. In the former, our laws insist upon effective competition; in the latter, because we substantially confer a monopoly by limiting competition, we must regulate their services and rates. The rigid enforcement of the laws applicable to both groups is the very base of equal opportunity and freedom from domination for all our people, and it is just as essential for the stability and prosperity of business itself as for the protection of the public at large. Such regulation should be extended by the Federal Government within the limitations of the Constitution and only when the individual States are without power to protect their citizens through their own authority. On the other hand, we should be fearless when the authority rests only in the Federal Government....

The United States fully accepts the profound truth that our own progress, prosperity and peace are interlocked with the progress, prosperity and peace of all humanity. The whole world is at peace. The dangers to a continuation of this peace today are largely the fear and suspicion which still haunt the world. No suspicion or fear can be rightly directed toward our country.

Those who have a true understanding of America know that we have no desire for territorial expansion, for economic or other domination of other peoples. Such purposes are repugnant to our ideals of human freedom. Our form of government is ill adapted to the responsibilities which inevitably follow permanent limitation of the independence of other people. Superficial observers seem to find no destiny for our abounding increase in population, in wealth and power except that of imperialism. They fail to see that the American people are engrossed in the building for themselves of a new economic system, a new social system, a new political system — all of which are characterized by aspirations of freedom of opportunity and thereby are the negation of imperialism. They fail to realize that because of our abounding prosperity our youth are pressing more and more into our institutions of learning; that our people are seeking a larger vision through art, literature, science, and travel; that they are moving toward stronger moral and spiritual life — that from these things our sympathies are broadening beyond the bounds of our Nation and race toward their true expression in a real brotherhood of man. They fail to see that the idealism of America will lead it to no narrow or selfish channel, but inspire it to do its full share as a nation toward the advancement of civilization. It will do that not by mere declaration but by taking a practical part in supporting all useful international undertakings. We not only desire peace with the world, but to see peace maintained throughout the world. We wish to advance the reign of justice and reason toward the extinction of force.

Inaugural Address, Washington, D.C., March 4, 1929
(from book, The State Papers and
Other Public Writings of Herbert Hoover)

Before arriving in Washington, Mrs. Hoover bought a comfortable colonial house with an acre of garden overlooking a large part of the city, at 2300 S Street, which was to be our home for eight years. And again, for the fifth time in our twenty-two years of married life, she was to run a different house with her usual good taste and economy. She soon transformed the garden into charming order. For two-thirds of the year, it was bright with flowers. It contained several great oaks, survivors of the primeval forest which had

Rigid justice
is the basis of all
ordered liberty . . .

President Hoover called for voluntary effort
to end the depression at an October, 1930, appearance before
the American Federation of Labor convention.

Presidents cannot always kick
unscrupulous persons out the door . . .

covered the site of Washington. She built a large porch at the rear of the house where we had meals out-of-doors during the warm months. The boys attended the Friends' School, the Western High School, and the Palo Alto High School before entering Stanford. Both Mrs. Hoover and I believed that these public schools were a better prelude to American life than many private schools.

Herbert was now eighteen and ready to enter Stanford. During his vacation, he secured jobs at manual labor — an invaluable part of education. Allan was still in the stage of adventure where all sorts of animals must be accumulated. By providing food and water for the birds, he induced scores of them daily to visit us. He also provided them quarters by hanging gourds in the trees. Two dogs and two cats were necessary, and among the transitory possessions were two ducks which he trained to sit on the front porch to the infinite entertainment of passers-by. A selection of land turtles gathered from the woods was all right; but two small alligators, presented to him by Clarence Woolley, were somewhat of a trial, for Allan believed they must be bedded at night in the bathtubs.

From book, The Memoirs of Herbert Hoover:
The Cabinet and the Presidency (1920-1933), *1951, 1952*

To Mrs. Hoover, her position must be the symbol of everything wholesome in American life. She was oversensitive, and the stabs of political life which, no doubt, were deserved by me hurt her greatly. She was deeply religious, and to her such actions were just plain wickedness. Her only departures from sweet urbanity were in outrage at some unfairness in our opponents — and that in private. I suggested to her one time that a good reason for holding to orthodox religious faith was that it included a hot hell, and that she could console herself that this kind of politician and writer who escaped retribution in this world would find special facilities in the world to come. But she was too gentle a soul to see any humor in my idea.

She had a warm intuition, and she instinctively studied every new person who came into our orbit. Of those who were likely to be more than casual passers-by, she unobtrusively collected a great deal of background. Except where she felt it imperative, she never

volunteered her judgments. However, I could tell them from her expression. To her, moral standards were infinitely more important than intellectual qualifications. But Presidents cannot always kick evil-minded persons out of the front door. Such persons are often selected by the electors to represent them. She used to worry a good deal privately as to the devilment they might do to me. Loyalty to a cause, to a party, to a leader were part of her moral standards, and her judgment on these inherent qualities in persons at times proved uncanny.

From book, The Memoirs of Herbert Hoover:
The Cabinet and the Presidency (1920-1933), *1951, 1952*

It is now over 60 years since the Negro was released from slavery and given the status of a citizen in our country whose wealth and general prosperity his labor has helped create. The progress of the race within this period has surpassed the most sanguine hopes of the most ardent advocates. No group of people in history ever started from a more complete economic and

Before the era of
Presidential helicopters, pilot Harold
Pitcairn landed his autogyro on the White
House lawn to greet President Hoover.

A significant step to reduce military armaments was taken in July, 1930,
when President Hoover signed the London Naval Treaty.

cultural destitution. The fiftieth anniversary of the founding of Tuskegee marks at the same time almost the semi-centennial of Negro progress. Within that period the race has multiplied its wealth more than 130 times, has reduced its illiteracy from 95 per cent to 20 per cent, and reduced its death rate by one-half. It has risen to the ownership of more than 750,000 homes, has accumulated property to the value of billions, has developed a far-reaching internal network of social, religious, and economic organizations for the continued advancement of its people, has produced leadership in all walks of life that for faith, courage, devotion, and patriotic loyalty ranks with all the other groups in our country.

The greatest single factor in the progress of the Negro race has been the schools, private and public, established and conducted by high-minded self-sacrificing men and women of both races and all sections of our country, maintained by the states and by private philanthropy, covering the whole field of education from primary school through to college and university.

Radio Address, 50th Anniversary of Founding
of Tuskegee Institute, Apr. 14, 1931
(from book, The State Papers and
Other Public Writings of Herbert Hoover)

The difficulties of the agricultural industry arise out of a multitude of causes. A heavy indebtedness was inherited by the industry from the deflation processes of 1920. Disorderly and wasteful methods of

marketing have developed. The growing specialization in the industry has for years been increasing the proportion of products that now leave the farm and, in consequence, prices have been unduly depressed by congested marketing at the harvest or by the occasional climatic surpluses. Railway rates have necessarily increased. There has been a growth of competition in the world markets from countries that enjoy cheaper labor or more nearly virgin soils. There was a great expansion of production from our marginal lands during the war, and upon these profitable enterprise under normal conditions can not be maintained. Meanwhile their continued output tends to aggravate the situation. Local taxes have doubled and in some cases trebled. Work animals have been steadily replaced by mechanical appliances, thereby decreasing the consumption of farm products. There are many other contributing causes.

The general result has been that our agricultural industry has not kept pace in prosperity or standards of living with other lines of industry....

The most progressive movement in all agriculture has been the upbuilding of the farmer's own marketing organizations, which now embrace nearly two million farmers in membership and annually distribute nearly $2,500,000,000 worth of farm products. These organizations have acquired experience in virtually every branch of their industry, and furnish a substantial basis upon which to build further organization. Not all these marketing organizations are of the same type, but the test of them is whether or not they are farmer owned or farmer controlled. In order to strengthen and not to undermine them, all proposals for governmental assistance should originate with such organizations and be the result of their application. Moreover, by such bases of organization the Government will be removed from engaging in the business of agriculture.

Message to 71st Congress, Apr. 16, 1929
(from book, The State Papers and
Other Public Writings of Herbert Hoover)

. . . The basic question [concerns] the understanding, the ideals, the relationship of the individual citizen to the law itself. It is in this field that the press plays a dominant part. It is almost final in its potency to arouse the interest and consciousness of our people. It can destroy their finer sensibilities or it can invigorate them. I am well aware that the great majority of our important journals day by day give support to these high ideals.

I wonder, sometimes, however, if perhaps a little more support to our laws could not be given in one direction. If, instead of the glamour of romance and heroism, which our American imaginative minds too frequently throw around those who break the law, we would invest with a little romance and heroism those thousands of our officers who are endeavoring to enforce the law, it would itself decrease crime. Praise and respect for those who properly enforce the laws and daily condemnation of those who defy the laws would help. Perhaps a little better proportioned balance of news concerning those criminals who are convicted and punished would serve to instill the fear of the law.

I need not repeat that absolute freedom of the press to discuss public questions is a foundation stone of American liberty. I put the question, however, to every individual conscience, whether flippancy is a useful or even legitimate device in such discussions. I do not believe it is. Its effect is as misleading and as distorting of public conscience as deliberate misrepresentation. Not clarification, but confusion of issues arises from it.

Our people for many years have been intensely absorbed in business, in the astonishing upbuilding of a great country, and we have attempted to specialize in our occupations, to strive to achieve in our own specialties and to respect competency of others in theirs. Unconsciously, we have carried this psychology into our state of mind toward government. We tend to regard the making of laws and their administration as a function of a group of specialists in government whom we hired for this purpose and whom we call public servants. After hiring them it is our purpose casually to review their actions, to accept those which we approve, and to reject the rest.

This attitude of mind is destructive of self-government, for self-government is predicated upon the fact that every responsible citizen will take his part in the creation of law, the obedience to law, and the selection of officials and methods for its enforcement.

Address to Associated Press Luncheon, New York, New York, Apr. 22, 1929
(from book, The State Papers and
Other Public Writings of Herbert Hoover)

But peace is not a static thing. To maintain peace is as dynamic in its requirements as is the conduct of war. We can not say "Let there be peace" and go about other business. Nor are the methods by which peace is to be maintained and war prevented to be established by slogans or by abstract phrases or by academic theory. . . .

Armistice Day Address, Washington, D.C., Nov. 11, 1929
(from book, The State Papers and
Other Public Writings of Herbert Hoover)

Today, as never before in peace, new life-destroying instrumentalities and new systems of warfare are being added to those that even so recently spread death and desolation over the whole continent of Europe. Despite those lessons every government continues to increase and perfect its armament. And while this progress is being made in the development of the science of warfare, the serious question arises — are we making equal progress in devising ways and means to avoid those frightful fruits of men's failures that have blotted with blood so many chapters of the world's history?

Memorial Day Address, Arlington National Cemetery, Virginia, May 30, 1929 (from book, The State Papers and
Other Public Writings of Herbert Hoover)

President Hoover with his military aides at his 1930 Presidential New Year's reception.

To maintain peace is as dynamic in its requirements as the conduct of war...

With view to giving strength to the present economic stituation and providing for the absorption of any unemployment which might result from present disturbed conditions, I have asked for collective action of industry in the expansion of construction activities and in stabilization of wages. As I have publicly stated, one of the largest factors that can be brought to bear is that of the energetic yet prudent pursuit of public works by the Federal Government and state municipal and county authorities.

Telegram to State Governors, Nov. 23, 1929
(from book, The State Papers and Other Public Writings of Herbert Hoover)

What I have tried to do during these years has been to save the American people from disaster. They do not know what they have missed. Because they don't know what they have missed, they are dissatisfied with what has been done. In such circumstances, they turn to other leaders.

A former European official recently observed that statesmen, in trying to prevent disaster, kill themselves off. He might say that my tactics have been wrong, that I should have waited until the American people were half-drowned and then have waded in and tried to save them. In such an event, they would, of course, have known what it was all about. But it would have meant catastrophe!

From book, Hoover Off the Record, *by Theodore Joslin, 1934*

Our civilization is much like a garden. It is to be appraised by the quality of its blooms. In degrees as we fertilize its soil with liberty, as we maintain diligence in cultivation and guardianship against destructive forces, do we then produce those blossoms, the fragrance of whose lives stimulate renewed endeavor, give to us the courage to renewed effort and confidence of the future.

On the 50th Anniversary of Thomas Edison's Invention of the Electric Lamp,
Dearborn, Michigan, Oct. 21, 1929
(from book, The State Papers and Other Public Writings of Herbert Hoover)

The recent crash...has caused the throwing of people out of work temporarily. It, in turn, has resulted in reduced consumption of capital goods, of luxuries and to some extent of necessities. Apprehension and fear are what we have to combat, among bus-

During naval maneuvers off the Virginia coast, President Hoover inspected sailors on the battleship U.S.S. Arizona.

iness that it will lose markets and among the poor that they will lose their jobs....

Ninety per cent of our difficulty in depressions is caused by fear.

From book, Hoover Off the Record, *by Theodore Joslin, 1934*

Fighting this depression is becoming more and more like waging a war. We have the combats, if against an unseen foe of inestimable strength. We have our men and we have our casualties among them. What we need most of all is generals. The need of them is as great today as in any war in which we have ever been engaged. I have some good ones. I need some more.

From book, Hoover Off the Record, *by Theodore Joslin, 1934*

In the large sense the primary cause of the Great Depression was the war of 1914-1918. Without the war there would have been no depression of such dimensions. There might have been a normal cyclical recession; but, with the usual timing, even that readjustment probably would not have taken place at that particular period, nor would it have been a "Great Depression."

From book, The Memoirs of Herbert Hoover: *The Great Depression (1929-1941), 1952*

Those who contended that during the period of my administration our economic system was one of *laissez faire* have little knowledge of the extent of government regulation. The economic philosophy of *laissez faire,* or "dog eat dog," had died in the United States forty years before, when Congress passed the Interstate Commerce Commission and the Sherman Anti-Trust Acts.

From book, The Memoirs of Herbert Hoover: *The Cabinet and the Presidency (1920-1933), 1951, 1952*

This is not an issue as to whether people shall go hungry or cold in the United States. It is solely a question of the best method by which hunger and cold shall be prevented. It is a question as to whether the American people on one hand will maintain the spirit of charity and mutual self help through voluntary giving and the responsibility of local government as distinguished on the other hand from appropriations out of the Federal Treasury for such purposes. My own conviction is strongly that if we break down this sense of responsibility of individual generosity to individual and mutual self help in the country in times of national difficulty and if we start appropriations of this character we have not only impaired something infinitely valuable in the life of the American people but have struck at the roots of self-government. Once this has happened it is not the cost of a few score millions but we are faced with the abyss of reliance in future upon Government charity in some form or other. The money involved is indeed the least of the costs to American ideals and American institutions.

Press Statement, Washington, D.C., Feb. 3, 1931
(from book, The State Papers and Other Public Writings of Herbert Hoover)

We are upon the eve of the celebration of the two hundredth anniversary of the birth of George Washington. It is, therefore, appropriate that our observance of Memorial Day should this year be at this place, so intimately associated with the moral grandeur of the Father of Our Country.

This national shrine needs no description; the events enacted here require no recounting to the American people. The very name, Valley Forge, swells within us a pride of nationality. These peaceful fields hold a glory peculiarly their own. The sufferings of Washington's Army in that dreadful winter of privation have made this place famous among all men.

It was not the glory of battle for which these fields are remembered. No great battle was fought here. It was not the pomp of victory, for no martial triumph was won here. It was not the scene where peace was signed but which independence of a great nation was won. It was not the tombs of courageous men who, facing the enemy, gave the supreme sacrifice for their country to which we bow in reverence. A thousand other fields mark the courage, the glory, the valor, the skill, the martial triumph of our race. Yet the instinct and the judgment of our people after the abrasion of the years has appraised this place as a foremost shrine in the War of Independence and in our Nation. It is a shrine to the things of the spirit and of the soul....

This peculiar significance of Valley Forge in our American annals should strike us all with especial force in this particular moment of our national life. The American people are going through another Valley Forge at this time. To each and every one of us it is an hour of unusual stress and trial. You have each one your special cause of anxiety. So, too, have I. The whole Nation is beset with difficulties incident to a world-wide depression. These temporary reverses in the march of progress have been in part the penalty of excesses of greed, of failure of crops, and the malign inheritances of the Great War and a storm of other world forces beyond our control. Their far-reaching effects have fallen heavily upon many who were in no wise concerned with their causes. Many have lost the savings of a lifetime, many are unemployed, all know the misgivings of doubt and grave concern for the future.

No one who reviews the past and realizes the vast strength of our people can doubt that this, like a score of similar experiences in our history, is a passing trial. From it will come a greater knowledge of the weaknesses of our system, and from this knowledge must come the courage and wisdom to improve and strengthen us for the future.

Memorial Day Address, Valley Forge, Pennsylvania, May 30, 1931
(from book, The State Papers and Other Public
Writings of Herbert Hoover)

There are few men of the West of my generation who did not know the pioneer woman in his own mother, and who does not rejoice to know that her part in building that great civilization is to have such beautiful recognition. It was those women who carried the refinement, the moral character and spiritual force into the West. Not only they bore great burdens of daily toil and the rearing of families, but they were intent that their children should have a chance, that the doors of opportunity should be open to them. It was their insistence which made the schools and the churches.

Radio Address, Unveiling of the "Pioneer Woman" statue at
Ponca City, Oklahoma, Washington, D.C., Apr. 22, 1930
(from book, The State Papers and Other Public
Writings of Herbert Hoover)

The instinct of our people with the passing of time sifts out those men and those events and those places which become the marks on the national road of progress. The stone and the marble of all of our great national shrines are more than physical reminders of the mighty past of our country and the great deeds of America. They are symbols of things of the spirit. . . .

No man gazes upon the tomb of Lincoln without reflection upon his transcendent qualities of patience, fortitude, and steadfastness. The very greatness which history and popular imagination have stamped upon him sometimes obscures somewhat the real man back of the symbol which he has become. It is not amiss to reflect that he was a man before becoming a symbol. To appreciate the real meaning of his life we need to contemplate him as the product of the people themselves, as the farm boy, the fence builder, the soldier, the country lawyer, the political candidate, the legis-

Pioneer women helped build a great civilization . . .

President Hoover praised the part played by women in building the West at the dedication of the Pioneer Woman statue at Ponca City, Oklahoma, in 1930.

lator, and the President, as well as the symbol of union and of human rights.

Time sifts out the essentials of men's character and deeds, and in Lincoln's character there stands out his patience, his indomitable will, his sense of humanity of a breadth which comes to but few men.

Dedication of Remodeled Lincoln Tomb, Springfield, Illinois, June 17, 1931
(from book, The State Papers and
Other Public Writings of Herbert Hoover)

I do not minimize the scientific gains of such expeditions [as Admiral Byrd's to the Antarctic], but the human values are so immediate and so universal in their effect that it may well be that they transcend the scientific service. Every hidden spot of the earth's surface remains a challenge to man's will and ingenuity until it has been conquered. Every conquest of such a difficult goal adds permanently to mankind's sense of power and security. Great explorers, therefore, do not merely add to the sum of human knowledge, but also they add immensely to the sum of human inspiration.

Presentation of Medal to Admiral Richard E. Byrd,
Washington, D.C., June 30, 1930
(from book, The State Papers and
Other Public Writings of Herbert Hoover)

The most dangerous animal in the United States is the man with an emotion and a desire to pass a new law. He is prolific with drama and the headlines. His is not the road to the fundamental advance of the liberty and the progress of the American people at this time in our history. The greatest antidote for him is to set him upon a committee with a dozen people whose appetite is for facts. The greatest catastrophe that could come to our country is that administration policies or legislation or voluntary movements shall be encouraged or enacted upon the basis of emotion, not upon facts and reason.

Address before Gridiron Club, Washington, D.C., Dec. 14, 1929
(from book, Hoover After Dinner)

This is not the first time I have visited the site of this great dam. And it does give me extraordinary pleasure to see the great dream I have long held taking form in actual reality of stone and cement. . . .

This dam is the greatest engineering work of its character ever attempted at the hand of man. Its height alone is nearly seven hundred feet, making it more than one hundred feet higher than the Washington Monument, and far higher than any other such construction ever undertaken.

Visit to Boulder Dam (later rededicated Hoover Dam),
Nevada, Nov. 12, 1932

Recently I made the suggestion that the time had come when men should renounce starvation of women and children as a weapon of war, not alone for humane considerations but to remove a constant impulse to increasing arms. I have suggested that its enforcement must rest upon the public opinion of the world. There has been an almost universal approbation from our own countrymen of that proposal because it represents the spirit of America. From abroad has come its approval by the leaders of a score of nations. There are discordant notes and discordant nations. The old fallacy has been again produced that making war more terrible will frighten nations to peace. War has become more terrible every year since the invention of gunpowder, and every half century has seen more and more men sacrificed upon the battle field. Human courage rises far above any terror yet invented. I have been told that one cannot furnish food to civilians without furnishing it to armies, but no body of armed men ever did starve when food existed. There was no army in the World War that did not feed in full up to the last hour of the armistice, no matter when rows of pinched faces and emaciated children stood by the roadsides and ransacked their offal for wasted bread.

I am instructed by some that by putting the screws on the civil population we get war over with more quickly and it is thus more humane; the last war proved that attempts at starvation only sharpen hate; it hardens resolution. I have been told that no advance rules made in peace can be made binding in war; that public opinion of the neutral world is futile to restrain belligerents when the war is once launched. That is partly true, unless the subject is one on which public opinion can instantly react as to right and wrong. Public opinion of the neutral world does not react on the legalistic question of whether doormats are contraband or noncontraband. That is the main reason why all the agreements providing for the so-called freedom of the seas have never become a reality. But public opinion can and will react against forced starvation of nations. I have seen it stated that public opinion of neutrals had no effect in the last war. On the contrary, when the final verdict of history is given, it will be found that the loser lost, not for lack of efficiency, or valor, or courage, or starvation, but by failure to heed the public opinion of what were originally neutral nations.

Public opinion against the use of starvation as a weapon once created will never be downed. The voice of America on behalf of humanity requires no agreement among nations to give it force. It needs no alliances, no leagues, no sanctions. That voice when raised in human cause is the most potent force in the world today.

Address before Gridiron Club, Washington, D.C., Dec. 14, 1929
(from book, Hoover After Dinner)

I will not go into the doctor's definition of an exhibitionist; suffice it to say they comprise those who have an abnormal desire to preen in public. One well-defined form is represented by those who visit the White House to say a hurried few words to the President and on leaving hand out a long statement to the reporters at the door on subjects that have never been or are little discussed with the President, but with the firm confidence that the implication of their visit will put them on page one, column one.

Address before Gridiron Club, Washington, D.C., Dec. 12, 1931
(from book, Hoover After Dinner)

I n any event the news release of a week ago describing what has taken place here tonight, contained description of a skit on White House censorship. That is a thorny subject, as old as the Government and involving the theory that the principal job of Presidents is to make news for both morning and afternoon editions each day, and particularly that it shall have a mixed flavor of human-interest story and a dog fight that will please the village gossips. A revered President, long since dead, once told me that there was no solution to this relation of the White House to the press; that there never would be a President who could satisfy the press until he was twenty years dead.

Let me say from some experience that the conduct of public business, both domestic and foreign, nine times out of ten is a matter of delicate negotiation, of long and patient endeavor to bring about the meeting of many minds. One critical essential in all such negotiations is to avoid the rock of announced positions and the inflammation of public controversy by which measures affecting men and nations may be wrecked before a common understanding may be reached through the long and tedious process of give and take. But naturally the correspondents, under pressure to discover every step of such processes and to envisage every difference of opinion in those terms of combat, to satisfy the village gossips, would require to have minute-by-minute access to the most confidential conversation (for both morning and evening editions) and to have mimeographed copies of all foreign dispatches. Not always having these facilities given to them they must satisfy the managing editor somehow at least by a column damning the Government for secrecy, with

forebodings and a dark conspiracy against public interest with Wall Street, or Downing Street, or some other dark alley. Yet if all of these facilities were offered minute-by-minute the press would be entirely upset because such facilities are of no importance unless given as individual scoop to the exclusion of every other newspaper.

Address before Gridiron Club, Washington, D.C., Dec. 12, 1931
(from book, Hoover After Dinner)

A third and more subtle purpose of the club appears to be that of careful and pointed instruction to Government officials and political leaders as to their errors and shortcomings. This instruction is enforced by the threatening gridiron which, like the traditional schoolroom switch, hangs here behind the teacher's desk. These educational facilities of the Gridiron Club thus include a regular and rigid enforcement by way of roasting. I am reminded of the annals of the early Christian Church, which contain the record of the singular case of one of the pioneer Christians. The man was zealous in the practice of the true faith, and for that reason became unpopular in his community. The citizens finally decided he was a nuisance and should be gotten rid of. Their methods were in accord with the custom of the times. Having no modern gridiron, they trussed him up at full length on a spit ordinarily used for roasting whole beeves and put him over a great bed of red-hot coals. They were careless, however, about turning the spit, with the result that the true Christian was roasted only on one side. He bore his sufferings with remarkable composure and good nature. But at last he felt moved to remark to his neighbors that he believed he was now thoroughly done on one side and would they mind turning him over.

Address before Gridiron Club, Washington, D.C., Dec. 10, 1932
(from book, Hoover After Dinner)

T he nature of the Presidential office as it has evolved through the history of the Republic is somewhat puzzling. Since the Founding Fathers, we had grown from 3,000,000 population to 135,000,000 and from thirteen to forty-eight states. We had grown from an agricultural country to a complex industrial nation. We had risen in power to the first stature among nations. The original constitutional concept of the President's office had certainly been enlarged. He had become a broader policy-maker in legislation, foreign affairs, economic and social life than the Founding Fathers ever contemplated.

The President is, by his oath, one of the protectors

President Hoover opened a White House business conference on his depression recovery program in August, 1932.

of the Constitution. As "Chief Executive" he is administrator of the government. As "Commander-in-Chief" he has a responsibility in national defense. As "Chief Magistrate" he is the chief Federal law enforcement officer. Through his responsibility for foreign relations, he must keep the peace in a world of increasing perplexities. With the growth of the two-party system, he has become the leader of his party, bearing the responsibility to carry out the platform on which he was elected and to keep the party in power. As adviser to the Congress on the state of the nation, he must demonstrate constant leadership by proposing social and economic reforms made necessary by the increasing complexity of American life. He must be the conserver of national resources, and he must carry forward the great public works in pace with public need. He must encourage all good causes. Presidents have given different emphasis to these functions, depending upon the man and the times. In the end the President has become increasingly the depository of all national ills, especially if things go wrong.

There has been an increasing ascendancy of the Executive over the Legislative arm, which has run to great excesses. The President's veto was not often used in the first seventy years of the Republic as legislative power but was held as a safeguard of constitutionality of legislation. Gradually this power of the veto has expanded until he possesses one-third of the legislative authority. Far from merely advising Congress, he is expected to blast reforms out of it. With the growth of the Federal expenditure the Congress has lost much of its control of the purse, the original citadel of parliamentary power.

I felt deeply that the independence of the Legislative arm must be respected and strengthened. I had little taste for forcing Congressional action or engaging in battles of criticism. However, this could not be avoided two years later when I had to deal with a Democratic Congress bent on the ruin of the administration.

From book, The Memoirs of Herbert Hoover: The Cabinet and the Presidency (1920-1933), *1951, 1952*

Robert Moses of New York once told me of an experience in ghost-written speeches. As a young reporter he had been attached to Mr. Hylan's campaign for Mayor of New York. Hylan had only one speech and that advocating a five-cent subway fare. As the campaign went on, the Mayor had repeated it in all parts of the city until it was worn out. Finally he asked Bob to write him a different speech. Bob was greatly flattered and worked diligently. The final sentence of the peroration was, "I call for the spirit of 1776." Hylan stumbled through the strange vocabulary and diction and finally braced himself for the last line — "I call for the spirit of one, seven, seven, six."

From book, The Memoirs of Herbert Hoover: The Cabinet and the Presidency (1920-1933), *1951, 1952*

About the most painful thing is to preserve the ego of that part of mankind which expects to be personally remembered by name. In a reception line in Chicago a lady said, "Don't you remember me?" and waited sternly for an answer. I try to be honest, so I

An independent Congress must be respected . . .

replied, "I am sorry, madam, but I would like to and no doubt could, if you will tell me where we met." She said rather indignantly, "Why, I sat on the end of the third row when you spoke in Indianapolis, and you looked right at me." Another trial of campaign life is the autograph. I am convinced that I have half a million in circulation. Certainly there is inflation in these issues.

From book, The Memoirs of Herbert Hoover: The Cabinet and the Presidency (1920-1933), *1951, 1952*

This campaign is more than a contest between two men. It is more than a contest between two parties. It is a contest between two philosophies of government.

We are told by the opposition that we must have a change, that we must have a new deal. It is not the change that comes from normal development of national life to which I object, but the proposal to alter the whole foundations of our national life which have been builded through generations of testing and struggle, and of the principles upon which we have builded the nation. The expressions our opponents use must refer to important changes in our economic and social system and our system of government, otherwise they are nothing but vacuous words. And I realize that in this time of distress many of our people are asking whether our social and economic system is incapable of that great primary function of providing security and comfort of life to all of the firesides of our 25,000,000 homes in America, whether our social system provides for the fundamental development and progress of our people, whether our form of government is capable of originating and sustaining that security and progress.

This question is the basis upon which our opponents are appealing to the people in their fears and distress. They are proposing changes and so-called new deals which would destroy the very foundations of our American system.

Our people should consider the primary facts before they come to the judgment — not merely through political agitation, the glitter of promise, and the discouragement of temporary hardships — whether they will support changes which radically affect the whole system which has been builded up by a hundred and fifty years of the toil of our fathers. They should not approach the question in the despair with which our opponents would clothe it.

Campaign Speech, Madison Square Garden,
New York, New York, Oct. 31, 1932

Our Government differs from all previous conceptions, not only in this decentralization, but also in the separation of functions between the legislative, executive, and judicial arms of government, in which the independence of the judicial arm is the keystone of the whole structure.

It is founded on a conception that in times of emergency, when forces are running beyond control of individuals or other cooperative action, beyond the control of local communities and of States, then the great reserve powers of the Federal Government shall be brought into action to protect the community. But when these forces have ceased there must be a return of States, local, and individual responsibility.

Campaign Speech, Madison Square Garden,
New York, New York, Oct. 31, 1932

We have heard a great deal in this campaign about reactionaries, conservatives, progressives, liberals, and radicals. I have not yet heard an attempt by any one of the orators who mouth these phrases to define the principles upon which they base these classifications. There is one thing I can say without any question of doubt — that is, that the spirit of liberalism is to create free men; it is not the regimentation of men. It is not the extension of bureaucracy.

Campaign Speech, Madison Square Garden,
New York, New York, Oct. 31, 1932

My fellow Californians: I am deeply moved by the reception I have had in coming to my own state. I have been absent now for nearly four years. Any Californian suffers a deprivation if he is away for so long a period from its hills and valleys and from people of his own kind. Nothing but the greatest national crisis we have ever met in peace time, nothing but the office to which you in California have elected me, would have held me so long from the refreshment of soul that comes to every man from these hills, valleys, and mountains and the people of California.

Campaign Speech, San Francisco, California, Nov. 8, 1932

You will expect me to discuss the late election. Well, as nearly as I can learn we did not have enough votes on our side. . . . My country has given me the highest honor that comes to man. . . . That is a debt I can never repay.

Only a few rare souls in a century, to whose class I make no pretension, count much in the great flow of this Republic. The life stream of this nation is the generations of millions of human particles acting under impulses of advancing ideas and national ideals gathered from a thousand springs. These springs and rills have gathered into great streams which have nurtured and fertilized this great land over the centuries. Its dikes against dangerous floods are cemented with the blood of our fathers. Our children will strengthen the dikes, will create new channels, and the land will grow greater and richer with their lives.

We are but transitory officials in government whose duty is to keep the channels clear and to strengthen and extend their dikes. What counts toward the honor of public officials is that they sustain the national ideals upon which are patterned the design of these channels of progress and the construction of these dikes of safety. What is said in this or in that political campaign counts no more than the sound of the cheerful ripples or the angry whirls of the stream. *What matters is — that God help the man or the group who breaks down these dikes, who diverts these channels to selfish ends. These waters will drown him or them in a tragedy that will spread over a thousand years.*

From book, The Memoirs of Herbert Hoover:
The Great Depression (1929-1941), 1952

Mrs. Hoover and I left the White House without regrets except that the job of recovery and some needed reforms were incomplete. We had no illusions that America would come to an end because we were going back home again. I had now been in almost full-time public service since 1914 — nineteen years. And during that time we had not lived at home for a total of more than a few scattered months. The mental taste of one's own gadgets and gardens was good.

Democracy is not a polite employer. The only way out of elective office is to get sick or die or get kicked out. Otherwise one is subject to the charge of being a coward, afraid to face the electorate. When a President is out he carries no pension,* privilege, nor pomp. He does not even carry away an honorary title, not even

---

* American ex-Presidents now receive a pension.

Governor, Judge, or Colonel. He is about the only retiring public official who is just Mister. He stands in line for a seat and for tickets just like other citizens.

When the British Prime Minister is defeated he may if he wishes receive a great title, he automatically draws a great pension, and everybody makes way for his Lordship.

But the American method is better. It emphasizes the equalities of its democracy. And an ex-President is not devoid of honor or advantages. He is naturally recognized everywhere because his picture has appeared in every print every day for years. To his misfortune the pictures are mostly the flashlight sort with their mechanistic absence of flattery and implications of a prison personality. But recognition brings honor. The proof is that an ex-President is high in the seeking of autograph hunters. And their appraisals of his relative importance are definite. One day a youngster demanded three autographs, which seemed to imply a generous compliment. I asked: "Why three?" "It takes two of yours to get one of Babe Ruth's."

The American treatment of an ex-President has other real advantages. He can just be himself. He can go and come without the restraint of representing a class or a symbol. Up to the time of this writing, I have traveled tens of thousands of miles alone or with Mrs. Hoover, have wandered in the slums of a score of cities, bought things in a thousand stores, visited hundreds of industrial works, been entertained in every sort of home from the roadside cottage to the greatest of establishments. And everywhere I received pleasant, often affectionate, greetings, never an offensive word — to my face.

It might be difficult for some families to adjust themselves to the abrupt drop from palace to cottage. And the White House is a palace more comfortable than that of most kings. Our family had long alternated between the luxury of great cities and the primitive living of world frontiers, so that this change was no bump. Indeed Mrs. Hoover and I found abundant compensations from being kicked out of a job after this nearly forty years of administrative responsibility and nineteen years of strenuous public service. There came a great sense of release. It was emancipation from a sort of peonage — a revolution back to personal freedom. It was a release not alone from political pressures but from the routines of twelve to fourteen hours of work seven days a week. Even mealtime had to be given over to the discussion of the problems of the day; the nights were haunted by the things that went wrong; the so-called vacations were tied to the telephone and telegraph or to the visitor who knew that now was the time to discuss his problem.

Therefore, for the first time in long memory, neither Mrs. Hoover nor I had to get up in the morning at the summons of a human or mechanical alarm clock with its shock into reality. Breakfast was to be had when we wanted it. We read the papers and listened to the radio after breakfast instead of between bites. We did it with complete detachment, for no longer did events so directly affect us as before.

From book, The Memoirs of Herbert Hoover: The Great Depression (1929-1941), *1952*

Our children will create new channels for the nation's life stream . . .

The Hoovers enjoyed children's visits to the White House. Here, three youngsters present a May Day flower basket to Mrs. Hoover.

V
The Elder Statesman:
DOMESTIC POLITICS AND THE CHALLENGES TO LIBERTY

A good many things go around in the dark besides Santa Claus.

Address to John Marshall Republican Club,
St. Louis, Missouri, Dec. 16, 1935

While I can make no claim for having introduced the term "rugged individualism," I should be proud to have invented it. It has been used by American leaders for over a half-century in eulogy of those God-fearing men and women of honesty whose stamina and character and fearless assertion of rights led them to make their own way in life.

From book, The Challenge to Liberty, *by Herbert Hoover, 1934*

Liberalism has been ever the exponent of peace among nations. It is the surest hope of peace. Not in a hundred years have the great democracies of the world gone to war with each other. Yet that same century has been splattered with blood from despotisms battling with each other, and from Liberal governments defending themselves against attacks by such nations. The most practical proposal of peace to the world has been the extension of self-government. Peoples are far less likely than authoritarian governments to start wars.

Modern despotism, in every case, has achieved its purpose by fanning the fires of Nationalism. To inflame hate, and to stir the sacred emotion of patriotism as a drug to liberty, is a favorite device of those who seek power. Their effect is to increase enormously the dangers of conflict.

From book, The Challenge to Liberty, *by Herbert Hoover, 1934*

Be it noted that even "temporary" dictatorships are achieved by the direct and emphatic promise to the people that their liberties eventually will be restored. In Russia, the theory runs that some liberty will be restored when the revolution of the proletariat is "con-summated." In Italy, liberties will be restored as the people earn them by faithful obeisance before the throne of Fascism. Under Naziism, liberties will be restored when the "National Consolidation" is secured.

A sobering commentary upon the processes of mass psychology is the idea in all of these countries that Liberty may be achieved and secured only by sacrifice of liberties to the efficiency of tyranny.

From book, The Challenge to Liberty, *by Herbert Hoover, 1934*

The abuses of Liberty fall naturally into two separate groups. First is the betrayal of public and private trust by individuals, and second are the problems of economic exploitation and domination which arise in modern business organization.

We have had heart-breaking betrayals of trust both in public and private life, mostly through crime or through loopholes in the law. Equally wicked and less known are those who have operated to destroy business and values of securities that they might profit from the losses of the people.

Such betrayals are not alone stealing of money. They injure the most precious faith that has ever come to a people — faith in Liberty.

From book, The Challenge to Liberty, *by Herbert Hoover, 1934*

The challenge to us is that the purpose of American life cannot be accomplished by the methods of Liberty and within the frame of a government that cannot itself infringe upon Liberty. . . .

Indeed one of the most profound questions and a test of any society is whether it possesses regenerative forces within itself to work out its own solutions. The oldest answer of Liberalism to even benevolent dictatorship has been that such benevolence and its supposed efficiency are not continuous; that the even succession of genius does not occur; and that a free society which evolves its own correctives and contains its own dynamic forces within itself may be at times less "efficient" but is the only society assured of permanence.

From book, The Challenge to Liberty, *by Herbert Hoover, 1934*

Bureaucracy has already developed a vast ramifying propaganda subtly designed to control thought and opinion. The constant use of the radio, the platform, and the press, by device of exposition, news and attack with one point of view, becomes a powerful force in transforming the nation's mentality and in destroying its independent judgment. Bureaucracy's instinctive defense to criticism is to color the information and news with its objectives rather than presenting a cold analysis of results. It goes further in resentment to criticism and attempts to meet it with denunciation. We witness this vituperative impatience from those who believe they are serving the common good. Critics are smeared by personal attack upon character or motives, not answered by sober argument.

From book, The Challenge to Liberty, *by Herbert Hoover, 1934*

The depression brought vividly to the surface many failures in American life, many weaknesses latent in the organization of the system, many wickednesses and abuses of Liberty. Some of them are far deeper than the depression. We witnessed tragedy after tragedy to American aspirations and ideals. Abuses of Liberty through betrayal of trust or through economic domination, whether they be called "unfair competition," special privilege, monopoly, exploitation, vicious speculation, or the use of property to oppress others, are all sins against the whole system and ideals of Liberty. Thoughtful men had long warned of these weaknesses, but the American people are slow to move by an abstraction. Here indeed has been the battleground of Liberty against oppression ever since the beginning of the Industrial Age. Upon our conceptions of duty, our courage, and our abilities will Liberty survive.

In the confusion of striving to overcome the depression, and the multitude of social and economic problems born of our progress and a wider vision of human betterment, the American System of Liberty has been

Hoover warned that the sacrifice of personal liberty would not bring economic security in a Constitution Day speech at San Diego, California, in 1935.

challenged and the cry has gone up that these problems cannot be solved within its own philosophy, and within a frame of government which cannot itself infringe upon Liberty. Here is indeed its real test.

From book, The Challenge to Liberty, *by Herbert Hoover, 1934*

... Modern revolutions do not necessarily imply civil war or the killing of people. They more often force back the weakened liberal institutions by clipping, bending, or atrophying of the old frameworks into new forms and purposes.

Revolution in government is a hard term to define. Too often we use it colloquially for normal change. Any definition of revolution in democracies implies something more than the peaceful fruition of their philosophies and ideals matured by honest discussion and submitted to the ballot. It means some violent wrench in the whole philosophy of a people — a wrench from their ideas and ideals whence sprang their institutions and their form of government. In many democratic states it has meant the imposition of a new philosophy, changed ideas and changed ideals without their open submission to the people, and often without the people recognizing its approach until it has become a reality. And not a few of these recent revolutions have been stimulated by ambitious men preying upon the suffering of humanity for personal power.

From book, The Challenge to Liberty, *by Herbert Hoover, 1934*

Nobody denies that there is a "right" to strike. But there are extremes at which any "right" becomes an oppression. There are legal limits even to the right of free speech. When the "right to strike" was fully accepted, strikes were believed to be solely pressures on employers to improve working conditions and wages. But a new idea has now grown up around the use of the strike: that this weapon can be employed for political and ideological purposes and that it can be used so to injure and endanger the people at large that in their misery they or the government will be forced to do the strikers' bidding. It is the people who suffer.

From article, "The Right to Strike,"
in This Week *magazine, Dec. 29, 1946*
(from book, Addresses Upon
the American Road 1945-1948)

This is the nth-plus-1 Commission on Organization of the Government in which I have participated in 33 years. Most of such Commissions have been set up by Presidents hopeful that the Congress would listen to the words of wisdom. ...

Last Monday, after some 18 months of hard work we got around to that remark in the law about elimination of those functions which are competitive with private enterprises. You may have noted that we found them in many agencies of the Government.

There appear to be somewhere between 2,000 and 3,000 of them. We have not had the time to dissect all of them.

When we came to look into the history of these Government business enterprises, we found most of them were created in wars and emergencies for some special needed task. But when the task was completed, each had aboard it an empire-seeking bureaucracy and a large pressure group which benefited from it. With these high inspirations, they developed an extraordinary longevity. One of them lasted 36 years and lost money nearly every year. Some of these enterprises are necessary; some are non-competitive.

Many of them in their accounts claim they earn a profit and are, therefore, a benevolent institution. But all of them are exempt from Federal taxes. Very few of them pay any interest or amortization of the capital the Government had invested in them. And many of them do not include overhead personnel in their expenditures, or pensions and other "fringe benefits." Also, they do not mention the increased taxes the Government would receive if the business were done by private enterprise. Naturally, they are joyous in the demonstration of their great capacity to compete with private enterprise. Our Commission made the remark that this was a strange proceeding in a Government pledged to fair competition.

New York, New York, May 19, 1955
(from book, Addresses Upon
the American Road 1955-1960)

Possibly I knew Robert A. Taft during his public life longer than any living person. But I never think of him as Robert. As with millions of Americans he was Bob to me. And, on this occasion, I shall speak of him as Bob as I have always done during the 36 years of our close friendship and deep affection.

When our country joined the First World War in 1917, Bob was rejected for service in the Army. Seeking some place for service, he joined the legal staff of the war organizations under my direction. That included not only service in Washington, but also service in Paris during the negotiations of the Treaty of Versailles. That great conference on the fate of the world was going on almost next door. Part of Bob's duties were to work with the American Delegation and, at

times, the delegations of other nations. Here began his
first experience in international conflicts.

In those overcrowded days in Paris, the principal
members of my staff and I dined together as the only
moment when we could consider our overall plans and
policies. On one of these dinner occasions, Bob joined
in with an impressive advocacy of the League of
Nations.

Robert A. Taft was an official with a social conscience.
He not only would not desert his post; he never deserted
his people.

Of course, he bore his cross. He was denounced as
an isolationist, as a reactionary, as an enemy of the
poor and a friend of the rich. These attacks never
shook him, because of his philosophy and moral attitude toward life. His conscience was always clear. He
was one who lost no sleep nights worrying that he would
be found out. He lost much sleep over the fate of his
country. He knew to the end that his was a moral attitude toward life and men and that he had given to his
country his last full measure of devotion.

Dedication of Robert A. Taft Memorial, Washington, D.C., Apr. 14, 1959
(from book, Addresses Upon the American Road 1955-1960)

*Modern revolutions
move quickly from concept
to reality . . .*

Two years after his 1932
campaign defeat, Hoover spoke to Stanford
University alumni in New York City.

This is the seventh time I have had the high honor of addressing the Conventions of the Republican Party. The last two times I have indicated I was making my farewell appearance. I have both a precedent and a request for this appearance. Some of you may recollect that the great singer of yesteryear, Madame Adelina Patti, by request came to America six times to make farewell appearances. But do not get too alarmed over the possibility of three more from me.

Republican National Convention, San Francisco, California, Aug. 21, 1956
(from book, Addresses Upon the American Road 1955-1960)

My good friends: Your reception is indeed a demonstration of great friendship. It kindles a great glow in my heart.

I had not expected to speak at this Convention. In each of your last three Conventions I bade you an affectionate good-bye. Apparently, my good-byes did not take. And I have been bombarded with requests to do it again for the fourth time. Unless some miracle comes to me from the Good Lord this is finally it.

Republican National Convention, Chicago, Illinois, July 25, 1960
(from book, Addresses Upon the American Road 1955-1960)

Former President Hoover addressed a group of Nebraska farmers in 1936. He asked the crowd to defend its heritage of individual liberty in the face of paternalistic government farm programs.

Unless some miracle comes from the
Good Lord, this is my final appearance ...

In an activity identified with former President Truman, Hoover and
his son, Allan, took an early morning stroll in New York City, in March, 1933.

VI
The Elder Statesman:
WAR, PEACE AND FAMINE

From the beginning of the Great War I saw the development of the propaganda directed at the United States from both sides. I was so impressed that I collected this material for years. The War Library at Stanford University holds stack after stack of this emanation from every government at war. And, in the light of what we now know really happened, it comprises the greatest collection of part lies on the face of the earth. It ought to be studied.

There are certain types of propaganda in motion today which fertilize our soil for our entry into war. For instance, one of these volleys of propaganda asserts that a great war in Europe is inevitable. That is a half-truth. The setup in Europe has made a general war inevitable every hundred years since the Romans kept the peace. And until mankind makes much greater progress it will continue to be inevitable. But the pounding in of that phrase is either sensational journalistic speculation or European propaganda of the preparatory type.

From book, Shall We Send Our Youth to War?,
by Herbert Hoover, 1939

The American people are today tense with anxiety lest they be led into another great war.

And some of our people seem to be accepting glib talk of war as if it were something more good than evil. Truly many years have already gone by since we ceased to feed boys to the cannon. It seems difficult to believe that only about one third of the living American people are old enough to remember the World War well.

We have urgent need today to recall the realities of modern war. And we have desperate need to take into our national thinking the gigantic yet invisible forces behind war which are again moving in Europe. . . .

First, let me say something from this experience of what war really is. Those who lived in it, and our American boys who fought in it, dislike to recall its terribleness. We dwell today upon its glories — the courage, the heroism, the greatness of spirit in men. I, myself, should like to forget all else. But today, with the world driving recklessly into it again, there is much we must not forget. Amid the afterglow of glory and legend we forget the filth, the stench, the death, of the trenches. We forget the dumb grief of mothers, wives,

and children. We forget the unending blight cast upon the world by the sacrifice of the flower of every race.

I was one of but few civilians who saw something of the Battle of the Somme. In the distant view were the unending trenches filled with a million and a half men. Here and there, like ants, they advanced under the thunder and belching volcanoes from 10,000 guns. Their lives were thrown away until half a million had died. Passing close by were unending lines of men plodding along the right side of the road to the front, not with drums and bands, but with saddened resignation. Down the left side came the unending lines of wounded men, staggering among unending stretchers and ambulances. Do you think one can forget that? And it was but one battle of a hundred.

Ten million men died or were maimed for life in that war. There were millions who died unknown and unmarked. Yet there are miles of unending crosses in a thousand cemeteries. The great monument to the dead at Ypres carries the names of 150,000 Englishmen who died on but a small segment of the front. Theirs was an inspiring heroism for all time. But how much greater a world it would be today if that heroism and that character could have lived.

And there was another side no less dreadful. I hesitate to recall even to my own mind the nightmares of roads filled for long miles with old men, young women, and little children dropping of fatigue and hunger as they fled in terror from burning villages and oncoming armies. And over Europe these were not just a few thousands, but over the long years that scene was enacted in millions.

From book, Shall We Send Our Youth to War?,
by Herbert Hoover, 1939

American soil has been treacherously attacked by Japan. Our decision is clear. It is forced upon us. We must fight with everything we have. I have opposed the foreign policies of our Government. I have believed alternative policies would have been better. But whatever our differences of view may be as to the causes which have led to this situation, those are matters to be threshed out by History. Today there is just one job before the American people. We must defeat this invasion by Japan and we must fight it in any place that will defeat it. Upon this job we must and will have unity in America. We must have and will have full support for the President of the United States in this war to defend America. We will have victory.

Press Statement, New York, New York, Dec. 8, 1941
(from book, Addresses Upon the American Road 1941-1945)

A few years ago in speaking from experience in the First World War, to the students of one of our universities, I said:

One of the emotions arising from that total war was rabid intolerance. National unity was essential in the face of national danger. But impatience of some people ran to intolerances which themselves brought limitations not only on free speech but on other liberties. The democratic governments did not need or did not want such violences. Intolerance did.

Our histories of that war teem with regrets over those attitudes and proofs that intolerance brought many material and spiritual losses. And above all that intolerance did not contribute to national unity.

I suppose it is asking too much that we would profit by this experience of the last war. But today intolerance at the hands of some self-appointed persons and organizations has already, in five months, risen to great heights. Perhaps it is because the radio has multiplied the voices. Perhaps it is because the logic of the new intolerance is mostly made of name calling.

New York, New York, May 20, 1942
(from book, Addresses Upon the American Road 1941-1945)

The Western world has seen these gigantic explosions into revolution, tumult and world war before. When the killing ceased, men met together, resolute upon making lasting peace. But always invisible forces have also sat at the peace table — both for good and evil.

The degenerations and emotions of world wars in many ways reach their most destructive point immediately after firing ceases.

Chicago, Illinois, Dec. 16, 1942
(from book, Addresses Upon the American Road 1941-1945)

There are those who propose to dismember defeated peoples into a multitude of states. That simply will not work, for the yearnings of racial solidarity are forces that will ultimately defeat any such idea. The history of periodically dismembered Germany is of intrigue and wars for unification that have disturbed the whole world. If we were defeated and our states separated, would we not conspire until we were united again?

Berton W. Crandall Photograph Collection

As an 86-year-old elder statesman, Hoover spent many informal moments in the library of his hotel suite in New York City.

Our experience is that indemnities such as Versailles imposed cannot be collected over a long term of years. There must be a terminal toward which the defeated peoples can look forward or they will constantly conspire.

The defeated countries after this victory can pay some indemnities, but if we are not to create anew the cesspools of world infection we must not attempt to hold them in bondage. That is not only vengeance — it is a delusion.

One of the greatest difficulties the world will have to meet when victory comes is the inevitable and universal emotional state. The hideous brutalities of the Axis

The vocal chords of democracy
are well trained for criticism . . .

An editorial cartoon gave tribute to
Hoover as President Truman's personal representative
for a world-wide food survey in the late 1940's.

powers will leave an ineradicable hate in millions of this generation. We cannot expect a growth of brotherhood in those who have suffered. Famine and poverty will have enveloped the whole world because of the Axis. Hate, revenge will be the natural emotions of all the peoples of the United Nations.

Unless the forces of fear, hate and revenge between peoples and nations can be turned aside, the world will again enter upon the ceaseless treadmill of war. By statesmanship at the end of this war, that hate, fear and revenge may ultimately decrease and die.

The enemy must be made to realize war does not pay. But if we want lasting peace, we must realize that nations cannot be held in chains. In the end there can be no trustworthy security except by giving the decent elements in a people a chance to cooperate in the work of peace.

From article, "History's Greatest Murder Trial," co-authored with Hugh Gibson, in This Week *magazine, Aug. 29, 1943 (from book,* Addresses Upon the American Road 1941-1945)

In 1928, as President-elect of the United States, I made a journey through the South American states. On that journey I made a number of public addresses in which I used the expression "the good neighbor policy." Following that journey I revised the previous attitude of the United States, declaring that the United States should never again intervene in a military fashion in Latin American states, that we should under no circumstances use force in support of claims of our citizens over their contracts or any other question. I emphasized this attitude throughout my administration by the withdrawal of the Marines from Nicaragua and the occupation troops from Haiti. I had the old Theodore Roosevelt interpretation of the Monroe Doctrine revised from the concept of right to interference into a declaration of Western Hemisphere solidarity, of freedom from old world encroachment. I am happy to say that was the last of these interventions and the last of American interferences in domestic policy of Latin American states.

Press Statement, New York, New York, Dec. 8, 1943 (from book, Addresses Upon the American Road 1941-1945)

Older men declare war. But it is youth that must fight and die. And it is youth who must inherit the tribulation, the sorrow, and the triumphs that are the aftermath of war.

Republican National Convention, Chicago, Illinois, June 27, 1944 (from book, Addresses Upon the American Road 1941-1945)

[I have been] asked . . . to say something on the theory and practice of personal liberty during the war. However when you are riding an earthquake there is a tendency to less interest in the theory of geology than to the more immediate practice.

We are in this war and the only road out of it is victory. There will be no liberty anywhere if we lose the war.

Inside America we are vibrating between two poles. We are fighting to preserve personal liberty in the world. Yet we must suspend part of it at home, in order to win. And suspension creates grave dangers because liberty rapidly atrophies from disuse. Vested interests and vested habits grow around its restrictions. It would be a vain thing to fight the war and lose our own liberties. If we would have them return we must hold furiously to these ideals. We must challenge every departure from them. There are just two tests: "Is this departure necessary to win the war?" "How are we going to restore these freedoms after the war?"

The exploration of these questions calls for a calm and philosophical disposition. And we have no right to complain. Our soldiers and sailors are deprived of all their freedoms except the right to grouse a little. But they will expect their freedoms back when they come home.

New York, New York, May 20, 1942 (from book, Addresses Upon the American Road 1941-1945)

While economic freedom must suffer most by the war, we can, if we will, and we must, keep the other great personal freedoms and their safeguards alive. Live free speech, free radio and free press are the heat that can thaw out any frozen liberties.

That there must be restraints upon speech and the press against information to the enemy needs no discussion. But there is left ample room to free speech and free press through pep-oratory and criticism of the conduct of the war. The only limit on pep speech, so far as I can see, is endurance of the audience. The use of free speech in criticism requires some limitations in war. Criticism is the higher art of protest. The vocal chords of democracy are well trained for this purpose. We start the practice of protest in the cradle and never let up.

And criticism of the conduct of the war is necessary if we are to win the war. We want the war conducted right. The margins between victory and defeat in our foreign campaigns are so narrow that if pressure groups are to take advantage of war to advance their interests,

We must live realistically with nations of different views . . .

Among Hoover's many honors was a scroll of appreciation for a "life of distinguished service to humanity" presented in 1949 by The Salvation Army in New York City.

or if we make blunders, or keep incompetent men in office, or allow corruption, bad organization and bad strategy, they can bring about defeat. Democracy can correct mistakes only through public exposure and opposition to them.

The President has unbelievable burdens in war; he deserves every support in this task. We cannot expect him to watch and direct the host of war agencies and officials that we must have to make war. The Congress and the people have to watch them.

The enemy may get mental comfort by reading these exposures and criticisms. But he will not get comfort from the remedy.

New York, New York, May 20, 1942
(from book, Addresses Upon the
American Road 1941-1945)

We must make up our minds to deal with governments and their social systems as they are and not as we should like them to be. On the United Nations' side in this war, we have a large variety of these systems. It is a dangerous fallacy to assume that more than a minor portion of the people in the world are democracies in our sense or that they ever will be in our lifetime. While we must hold to ideals of our own, it is entirely possible for us to work with nations which do not share our ideological views. We have to live and get along somehow in the same world. In fact, during the first fifty years of our existence, we were about the sole republic in a sea of kings or dictators. And for the most part we contrived to keep the peace with them.

It is of course easier to collaborate with some countries than with others, and we should make our plans accordingly. Honesty in facing these facts will save us much anguish.

From article, co-authored with Hugh Gibson
in Collier's *magazine, May, 1943*
(from book, Addresses Upon the
American Road 1941-1945)

There is another trend in our thinking that calls for correction. It arises from our weakness for simplification. Everybody knows that the world has shrunk in terms of communications. Melbourne and Calcutta are closer to us in flying hours than parts of our own country by train. Radio has made the spread of ideas general and instantaneous. But it is a long flying jump from that to the assumption that we now have one world in terms of political and social or philosophical and religious outlook.

Many naively assume that because Asia is now just over the horizon, Occidental and Oriental thought can be standardized. Or that they are consumed with a desire to adopt our way of life — to have the new world built on American blueprints.

All this is very interesting but it simply isn't true. We can test all this upon ourselves. Are we prepared to adopt Oriental philosophy, religion, economic standards or ways of life because we can more easily know their views and their way of living?

The fact is that the world remains pretty much as it has always been. We are only fooling ourselves by trying to distort a revolution in transport and communications into a world-wide political and social revolution. Though the skies be darkened with planes and the air filled with radio propaganda and messages of good will, life will go on much the same; Chinese and Italians, Americans, Arabs and Swedes will remain pretty much what they were. However beguiling the thought may be the world has not turned into a Great Melting Pot.

*From article, co-authored with Hugh Gibson
in* Collier's *magazine, May, 1943
(from book,* Addresses Upon the
American Road 1941-1945)

The sixth lesson of League [of Nations] experience was from the participation in all questions of the member nations, and thus the injection of members into the consideration of regional or even local problems which did not directly concern them. For instance, some 25 members were from the Western Hemisphere and Asia who were not concerned in the secondary problems of Europe. This system of world-wide representation resulted in the inability of the League to formulate major policies for peace in any one of the three great regions of the world. Most serious of all, it failed to formulate peace policies for Europe where it was most needed. As a matter of fact, the nations of Europe, to a very large extent, avoided the use of the League. That is evident in the fact that, during the effective life of the League, 19 important diplomatic conferences covering European questions took place in which the League had no part; 36 military alliances and nonaggression pacts were signed by member states which ignored the League; and 20 violent acts took place between nations where the League did not, or was not allowed to, take any action.

It is certain that very much better results can be obtained from a "world institution" under which the primary responsibility is divided regionally than from a world-wide organization which is charged with responsibility for the detailed problems of the whole earth. Experience indicates that the first step in the prevention of war is the development of regional policies and responsibilities.

Such a method would relieve the "world institution" of all except major world crises. It would, in our view, infinitely better serve to keep the peace. The view that there should be three major areas of Europe, Asia and the Western Hemisphere was advanced by the writers of these articles on May 1, 1942. Confirmation of these ideas has recently come from Mr. Churchill, who, on March 21, 1943, said:

"One can imagine that *under* a world institution embodying or representing the United Nations, and some day all nations, there should come into being a *Council of Europe* and a *Council of Asia.*

*From article, co-authored with Hugh Gibson
in* Collier's *magazine, June, 1943
(from book,* Addresses Upon the
American Road 1941-1945)

Senator Thomas of Utah: President Hoover.

Mr. Hoover: Senator, I do not believe there can be any doubt as to the general starvation amongst women and children in the occupied democracies. I do not believe there can be any doubt that relief could be given to those people, because of the experience in Greece and the fact that we are now delivering packages to prisoners in Germany under proper safeguards; and indeed, we are delivering packages to French, Belgian, Dutch and Norwegian military prisoners. At the moment, we are denying food to the children of those very prisoners. It seems to me they are as much in prison as are soldiers.

It does not seem to me that there can be any doubt that this question affects the whole future of Europe. It will be afflicted by a generation of stunted and diseased children and by the distorted minds that come up out of these miasmas.

Moreover, if we make no effort, it will affect our relations with those people for many years to come. For the last 2 years I have been steadily advocating that some effort should be made — that at least we should make a "try." I proposed a plan of procedure, and that plan was adopted as to Greece. The State Department has on numerous occasions certified that the Germans are receiving no benefits from the Greek relief and that it has saved the lives of millions of Greek women and children. The method now at least has had a demonstration.

In my original suggestions I proposed that the Swedes and the Swiss be asked to undertake this work, that they should be required to secure an agreement from the Germans that this food supply should be amply protected, that their ships should have immunity from attack and that they should have the right of complete supervision of distribution. That has been in progress in Greece now for nearly a year without any apparent failure.

It seems to me very urgent that we undertake it

now, even at this last moment — perhaps the last winter and the most disastrous winter that will overtake these people; that the least we could do would be to ask the Swedes and Swiss to see what arrangements they can make with the Germans; that, if they cannot make effective arrangements with them then, we will at least have discharged our responsibilities. If they succeed in making arrangements with the Germans such as they have made in respect of Greece and then the Germans should violate the agreements, we can withdraw it at any time and again have discharged our responsibilities.

Before Senate Subcommittee on Foreign Relations, Washington, D.C., Nov. 4, 1943
(from book, Addresses Upon the American Road 1941-1945)

We cannot hope for perfection at San Francisco.* In any event the Dumbarton Oaks press release does not purport to be the form of a treaty. It is a statement of methods. It must be drafted into precise terms. It is the height of wisdom that the people of the world should have a chance to see its final wording and to have a period in which to consider and even improve the agreement before it is signed. It will be more certain to last.

We do not have to hurry. If we take six years to make war it might be a good idea to take a few more months to build a sound organization to keep the peace. It was seven years from Yorktown to the Constitution.

Philadelphia, Pennsylvania, Apr. 17, 1945
(from book, Addresses Upon the American Road 1941-1945)

Let us examine what has happened to truth. It is the first fatality of any war. And total war results in the mass slaughter of truth. Propaganda is one of the weapons of war. And propaganda is at best but half truth. It tells only one side. Its justification is that strategy requires that the enemy be misled. Morale at home in war also requires a boost of spirit by suppression of some things and emphasis on others. War controls are used to cover up blunders and failures. Another taint of untruth still hangs heavy in the air. One of Lenin's principles of propaganda was to confuse vocabularies. At one time America had simple and well-understood expressions, such as self-government, independence of nations, democracy, personal freedom and liberalism. The war leaves us with these phrases stuffed with perversions of truth.

Exploitation of emotion, regimentation of the press and confusion are not operations in pure intellectual honesty. And these practices leave an imprint of the usefulness of lies. The consequence is that the habit of the war-perfected skills of government propaganda are carried over into peace. There is no national permanence in falsehood. There will be no lasting integrity in citizens unless there be intellectual honesty in government.

Chambersburg, Pennsylvania, Oct. 13, 1945
(from book, Addresses Upon the American Road 1945-1948)

The war has temporarily injured something in our ideals of justice. Our righteous indignations at the crimes which brought this war and the brutalities of the enemy have clouded our vision of justice.

Justice demands that the men responsible for this must be punished. It requires that the military castes and their weapons be destroyed and be kept destroyed.

But justice also requires that we do not visit on the children of millions of Germans and Japanese the sins of their fathers. Nor can we justly indict and punish two hundred million people. Vengeance and revenge are not justice. Measures which reduce the economic life of coming generations to the low levels of an agricultural state are neither justice nor good policy. That will create gigantic cesspools of hate, poverty and conspiracy against the world. There is no such thing as a "hard peace" or a "soft peace." It must be a just peace if we are to restore justice in the world. And without justice there is no peace.

Chambersburg, Pennsylvania, Oct. 13, 1945
(from book, Addresses Upon the American Road 1945-1948)

We have lost something in our sensitiveness to brutality. For instance, before the war we protested in deep indignation the bombing of children, women and civilian men by the Japanese at Nanking, the Russians at Helsinki, the Germans at Warsaw and London. We said wars must be confined to clashes of armed men, not the killing of civilians. Yet did we not wind up the war by killing tens of thousands of women and children at Hiroshima and Nagasaki? Even if we grant that it was necessary, it is not a matter to exult over.

Thousands of people are still being committed to concentration camps in Eastern Europe without a semblance of justice or compassion. Under the name of reparations men are being seized, and prisoners are being worked under conditions reminiscent of Roman slavery. Yet we have become so habituated to brutality that we are tolerating it with little protest.

Chambersburg, Pennsylvania, Oct. 13, 1945
(from book, Addresses Upon the American Road 1945-1948)

---

* From April through June 1945, 46 nations attended the United Nations Conference on International Organizations in San Francisco for the purpose of adopting the U.N. Charter.

I have been impressed by the vast difference in France, and especially in Italy, between the impressions gathered by casual visitors from the United States, who dine in black market restaurants and live in luxurious hotels, and the misery which the trained investigator finds when he leaves the tourist thoroughfares....

The American people should not be misled by reports of American travelers who judge the food supply of tens of millions of people by the kind of a meal that can be bought in a black market restaurant. Such meals cost from $2 to $5 per person. Even white-collar and skilled workmen in Italy and France earn less than $60 a month. Their entire pay for a month would support a family of five for only one or two days from such sources, and many of them are unemployed and without income. If our people are misled by such reports into slackening their efforts, it will be interpreted into the loss of from thousands to millions of human lives.

Radio Broadcast, Paris, France, Mar. 27, 1946
(from book, Addresses Upon the
American Road 1945-1948)

This is my report to the American people upon the world famine situation. Three weeks ago I broadcasted from Cairo our report upon the situation in Europe. Since then we have examined the food problems in Egypt, Iraq, India, Siam, the Philippines, China, Korea and Japan, thus compassing most of Asia.

I can therefore now consolidate our findings in twenty-five countries which we visited and upon several more upon which we have received competent information.

At the request of President Truman I have acted as a sort of Food Ambassador to determine needs; to discover possible further sources of supplies; and to coordinate the world's effort to master this danger to the lives of millions. Beyond this, it has been my duty to represent the solicitude of the American people and their desire to aid.

Along the 35,000 miles we have traveled, I have seen with my own eyes the grimmest spectre of famine in all the history of the world.

Of the Four Horsemen of the Apocalypse, the one named War was gone — at least for a while. But Famine, Pestilence and Death are still charging over the earth. And the modern world has added four more to this evil brigade. Their names are Destruction, Drought, Fear and Revolution. This crisis is not alone due to war destruction of agriculture. On the top of that calamity has been piled drought in the Mediterranean, drought in India, drought in China and partial drought in South Africa and the Argentine. Never

have so many evil Horsemen come all at one time.

Hunger hangs over the homes of more than 800,000-000 people — over one-third of the people of the earth. Hunger is a silent visitor who comes like a shadow. He sits beside every anxious mother three times each day. He brings not alone suffering and sorrow, but fear and terror. He carries disorder and the paralysis of government, and even its downfall. He is more destructive than armies, not only in human life but in morals. All of the values of right living melt before his invasions, and every gain of civilization crumbles. But we can save these people from the worst, if we will.

Chicago, Illinois, May 17, 1946
(from book, Addresses Upon the
American Road 1945-1948)

It may come as a great shock to American taxpayers that, having won the war over Germany, we are now faced for some years with large expenditures for relief for these people. Indeed, it is something new in human history for the conqueror to undertake.

Whatever the policies might have been that would have avoided this expense, we now are faced with it. And we are faced with it until the export industries of Germany can be sufficiently revived to pay for their food. The first necessity for such a revival is sufficient food upon which to maintain vitality to work.

Entirely aside from any humanitarian feelings for this mass of people, if we want peace; if we want to preserve the safety and health of our Army of Occupation; if we want to save the expense of even larger military forces to preserve order; if we want to reduce the size and expense of our Army of Occupation — I can see no other course but to meet the burdens I have here outlined.

Our determination is to establish such a regime in Germany as will prevent forever again the rise of militarism and aggression within these people. But those who believe in vengeance and the punishment of a great mass of Germans not concerned in the Nazi conspiracy can now have no misgivings, for all of them — in food, warmth and shelter — have been sunk to the lowest level known in a hundred years of Western history.

If Western civilization is to survive in Europe, it must also survive in Germany. And it must be built into a cooperative member of that civilization. That indeed is the hope of any lasting peace.

After all, our flag flies over these people. That flag means something besides military power.

Report to President Truman after European-Asian
Economic Mission, Feb. 26, 1947
(from book, Addresses Upon the
American Road 1945-1948)

65

As a former President, Hoover and his wife, Lou Henry,
returned to the garden of their Stanford home in 1940.

VII
The Elder Statesman:
FIGHTING THE COLD WAR

The dominant note in the world a year after World War I was hope and confidence; today it is fear and frustration. One year after the First World War we had signed peace; today there is no peace.

*Press Statement, Salt Lake City, Utah, Aug. 12, 1946
(from book,* Addresses Upon the
American Road 1945-1948)

What the world needs today is a definite, spiritual mobilization of the nations who believe in God against this tide of Red agnosticism. It needs a moral mobilization against the hideous ideas of the police state and human slavery. The world needs mobilization against this creeping Red Imperialism. The United States needs to know who are with us in the cold war against these practices, and whom we can depend on.

*Address to American Newspaper Publishers Association,
New York, New York, Apr. 27, 1950*

We should . . . coldly re-examine our experience from having fought two gigantic wars at fearful cost in resources and in lives. The valor of our men won great battles. But we have won no lasting peace. However, from these sacrifices we can deduce some vital truths.

I suggest to you a fundamental truism. War is justified only as an instrument for a specific consequence. That consequence for America was lasting peace. In four directions we strayed from that major objective.

First. Both wars proved that we cannot change ideas in the minds of men and races with machine guns or battleships. Our purposes were confused in both wars by crusades with glorious phrases about the personal freedom of man. Ideas in nations are rooted in their racial history, their very mores. Ideological wars are no more capable of settling anything than the thousand years of crusades and religious wars of the Middle Ages. Such wars have no ending and no victory. The way of life of a people must come from within; it cannot be compelled from without.

Whatever the present events may bring, I suggest we never again enter upon such crusades. If the Communist states like their slave ideology, we should engage in no loss of American lives to free them from it. Communism is a force of evil. It contains within itself the germs which will in time destroy it.

Radio Broadcast, Dedication of William Allen White Memorial,
Emporia, Kansas, July 11, 1950

Disarmament flows only from peace, not peace from disarmament.

New York, New York, Nov. 1, 1950

In South Asia and the Middle East we are witnessing vast readjustments of political power. Behind the solgan "Asia for the Asiatics" lie two centuries of the white man's exploitation. These forces have lighted a prairie fire of revolution against the West. They are removing the "white man's burden."

America had no part in this exploitation. Yet too often we find that many of these nations vote against the United States in the United Nations.

New York, New York, Jan. 27, 1952

Communism is an evil thing. It is contrary to the spiritual, moral and material aspirations of man. These very reasons give rise to my conviction that it will decay and die of its own poisons. But that may be many years away and, in the meantime, we must be prepared for a long journey.

New York, New York, Jan. 27, 1952

During my long years, I have participated in many world negotiations, which we hoped would promote peace. Today we have no peace.

From all this experience and now as the shadows gather around me, I may be permitted to make an observation and to offer a course of action.

Leaders of mankind have for centuries sought some form of organization which would assure lasting peace. The last of many efforts is the United Nations.

The time has come in our national life when we must make a new appraisal of this organization.

But first, let me say that I have, in all my official life believed in a world organization for peace. I supported the League of Nations when it was unpopular. I went down to defeat when, as President, I urged the Senate to join the World Court. I urged the ratification of the United Nations Charter by the Senate. But I stated at that time, "The American people should be under no illusions that the Charter assures lasting peace."

But now we must realize that the United Nations has failed to give us even a remote hope of lasting peace. Instead, it adds to the dangers of wars which now surround us.

The disintegrating forces in the United Nations are the Communist nations in its membership. . . .

In sum, they have destroyed the usefulness of the United Nations to preserve peace. . . .

More unity among free nations has been urged by President Truman, President Eisenhower, and President Kennedy. In cooperation with far-seeing statesmen in other free nations, five regional treaties or pacts have been set up for mutual defense. And there are bilateral agreements among other free nations to give military support to each other in case of attack. Within these agreements are more than forty free nations who have pledged themselves to fight against aggression.

Today, the menace of Communism has become world-wide.

The time is here when, if the free nations are to survive, they must have a new and stronger world-wide organization. For purposes of this discussion I may call it the "Council of Free Nations." It should include only those who are willing to stand up and fight for their freedom.

The foundations for this organization have already been laid by the forty nations who have taken pledges in the five regional pacts to support each other against aggression. And their are others who should join.

I do not suggest that the Council of Free Nations replace the United Nations. When the United Nations is prevented from taking action, or if it fails to act to preserve peace, then the Council of Free Nations should step in.

Address, Dedication of Herbert Hoover Library,
West Branch, Iowa, Aug. 10, 1962

*Disarmament flows only from peace,
not peace from disarmament . . .*

The Spanish influenced architecture at Stanford University in California frames the Hoover Tower,
part of the Hoover Institution on War, Revolution and Peace, a center for political science study.

VIII

THE PRIVATE MR. HOOVER

1919

My dear Betty,

I was glad to get your nice letter of August 3rd. I was in London then and it did not catch up with me until I got to Washington.

I am much astonished at Tippy's* fighting; it's not proper for small dogs; however, he may reform — they do that generally.

We have in our family

    2 small Boys
    1 Dog
    2 Cats
    11 Goldfish
    1 Canary
    3 Frogs
    14 Chickens
    2 Turtles
    1 Rabbit

And every morning 2 mice. They don't get through the day usually, as Allan needs the traps to catch more and thinks they should be drowned.

We also have 1,000,000 mosquitoes.

From book, On Growing Up, *by Herbert Hoover, 1949, 1959, 1962*

In 1938, I responded to many urgings by King Leopold, the Prime Minister, and many Belgian friends to revisit their country. It is of no purpose to describe the many courtesies extended to me by the King, the Ministry, the Parliament, and the thousands who lined the streets.

The most touching reminder of Relief days was a convening, for the first time in twenty years, of the C.R.B. and Comite National in our old Board room in a leading bank in Brussels. We had met there monthly to determine major policies until the American withdrawal when we declared war. With Belgian meticulousness, the chairs at the Board table had been marked for each member. After the final meeting dissolving the Comite in 1919, we had never met again, even for social purposes.

---

* Tippy was a dog that Mr. and Mrs. Hoover had given to Betty, the daughter of a man who had been an associate of Mr. Hoover's in the Food Administration.

On my visit to Belgium in 1938, the Vice-President of the Comite National Emmanuel Janssen, and the Secretary, Firmin Van Bree, summoned a special meeting, with the exact old protocol, at the Comite's former meeting hour and place. Of the Americans, Hugh Gibson, now Ambassador to Belgium, Hallam Tuck, Perrin Galpin, Millard Shaler, Milton Brown, and I were present.

The Chairman declared that the agenda for the day contained only three items — to call the roll, to honor the dead, and to renew friendships built in time of trial.

I have seldom been more affected than by that roll call and the frequent reply of the clerk, "Passed beyond." More than one-half of the chairs were empty. Many of the chairs were occupied by men obviously feeble with age, all of them under great emotion at so vivid a reminder of those who had passed on.

It was then I realized that while I had been in my early forties during the war, our Belgian colleagues had been old and tried men, often twenty years my senior.

Every article in the room and every word revived memories of men who had risen to great acts and great days. Somehow, a great spirit flowing with human devotion flooded the room.

From book, An American Epic, *by Herbert Hoover, 1959*

The reconstructed blacksmith shop of Hoover's father, Jesse, in Hoover Park at West Branch, Iowa.

Phil McCafferty

Christmas 1938

With Good Wishes for Christmas 1939
Herbert Hoover
Peggy II   *Herbert II*
Coby   *Joan*
Herbert III   *Peggy I*
Paul I   *LouHenry*
                Allan II
                his mark

The Hoovers' 1939 Christmas card
showed the entire family around the table at
the former President's Stanford home.

The interior of the Hoover birthplace
home at West Branch, Iowa. The wall clock
was stopped at 9:25, the exact
time of Hoover's death.

Fighting is not proper for small dogs,
but they will reform . . .

Hoover appreciated animals of all types. Here he posed with his dog at
his Washington, D.C., home before the 1928 Presidential election.

*A boy learns
certain moral precepts from
sportsmanship, but he
also needs a firm faith . . .*

There are two jobs for American boys today. One is being a boy. The other is growing up to be a man. Both jobs are important. Both are packed with excitement, great undertakings, high adventure.

Sometimes a boy's elders seriously interfere with his sheer joy in being a boy. They fill the department of growing up to be a man with grief and trouble. They create daily problems about everything: about health, about being made to eat food that is "good for you," washing around neck and ears, keeping neat, with special unreasonableness about rusty jack-knives and prized collections of snakes and toads.

There is a constant check-up to make sure that a boy's every waking activity is a constructive joy, not destructive glee. There is moral and spiritual instruction. And there is going to school. There are many disciplines, directions, urgings and pleadings from elders that no boy understands until he has become a man himself.

But then he looks backward to the enchanted boy's world in which he once lived so splendidly. And he finds its memory one of his most precious personal possessions.

I was a boy in the days before our civilization became so perfect, before it was paved with cement and made of bricks. Boys were not so largely separated from Mother Earth and all her works. And that was before the machine age denied them their natural right as primitive, combative animals to match their wits with bird and animal and insect.

*From article, "Enchanted World,"
in* This Week *magazine, Aug. 1, 1943
(from book,* Addresses Upon the
American Road 1941-1945)

Our civilization has made a difficult environment for these boys by covering their world with bricks and cement. We have equipped it with trucks, cabs, lamp posts and policemen. And we have constantly increased the number of boys per acre in these spots. To me, as a boy who grew up ranging the fields, tracking the rabbits and prairie chickens with the help of an unregistered mutt, these places in our cities are particularly depressing. There boys must go to pavements to find air supply, constructive joy or destructive glee.

The need for their education and the law require that they go to school six or seven hours a day, five days a week. But they must go to the pavements for evenings, weekends, and holidays and vacations.

These boys, like all boys and their sisters, are somebody's most precious possession. A boy presents joy, hopes and especially paradoxes. He strains our nerves, yet he is a complex of cells teaming with affection. He is a periodic nuisance. He is a part-time incarnation of destruction, yet he radiates sunlight to all the world and can become a joy forever. At times he seems the child of iniquity, yet generation by generation he pro-

Of all outdoor activities, Hoover enjoyed fishing the most. Here he casts into a wooded stream near Barnard, Vermont, in 1935.

72

duces a great nation.

A boy has two jobs: one is just being a boy, the other is growing up to be a man. Therefore, we better start our discussion by a diagnosis of what these boys are made of and what they need besides parents, food, clothes, a bed and the pavements.

First: He has an unbelievable amount of dynamism in his muscles and is equipped with a complete self-starter. With his impelling desire to take exercise, what he will do next is unpredictable. He needs to exhaust these surplus energies in an indestructible place.

Second: He has an insatiable curiosity. At times he seems to be the incarnation of an illuminated interrogation point. That requires that his newly discovered world be explored all over, including remote ideas. He needs a place for adventure without the use of brickbats.

Third: He is born with a large supply of imagination. He needs a chance to enter the land of make believe.

Fourth: He is an affectionate being. He needs companionship and friendship.

Fifth: He has a yen for battle, strife and competi-

While President, Hoover substituted a deep-sea pole for his favored fly rod to catch a sailfish during a Florida fishing trip.

tion. That battle instinct needs to be channeled into constructive competition with due recognition of his prowess.

Sixth: He wants to belong to something. The delinquency minded gang is at his door step. That danger needs to be diverted to a team of sports.

Seventh: He likes to play games. He needs every implement from checkers to a baseball bat.

Eighth: He takes to water and should have a periodic bath. The summer spray of hydrants by friendly firemen or dives into the muck around the docks is not the answer. He needs a sanitary swimming pool open the year around.

Ninth: He is often musical. He needs instruments all the way from a mouth organ to a violin.

Tenth: He is equipped with all the known physiological organs. They need to be periodically inspected by a doctor.

Eleventh: He has a sense of orderly conduct, or he can be instilled with it. That needs a place to try his hand in the problems of self-government.

Twelfth: He must some day learn a skilled occupation at which he can earn a living. He needs a chance to taste many trades in shops that are equipped and under the guidance of friendly workmen to find his occupational bent.

Thirteenth: He is an American citizen from birth. He needs to be sprinkled with its responsibilities, devotion to the flag and information about Karl Marx.

Fourteenth: He has a soul, and it needs moral and spiritual guidance. And in the land of sportsmanship he can learn moral precepts which are second only to those from religious faith.

Fifteenth: He comes from every race, color and religion. He needs a place to go where the dignity of all of them is respected.

Address at 50th Anniversary Banquet of the Boy's Clubs of America, New York, New York, May 10, 1956 (from book, Addresses Upon the American Road 1955-1960)

Although all men are equal before fish, there are some class distinctions among them. The dry-fly devotees hold themselves a bit superior to the wet-fly fishermen; the wet-fly fishermen, superior to the spinner fishermen; and the spinners, superior to the bait fishermen. I have noticed, however, that toward the end of the day when there are no strikes, each social level collapses in turn down the scale until it gets some fish for supper.

From book, Fishing for Fun — and to Wash Your Soul, *by Herbert Hoover, 1963*

A fisherman must be of contemplative mind, for it is often a long time between bites. Those interregnums emanate patience, reserve, and calm reflection — for no one can catch fish in anger, or in malice. He is by nature an optimist or he would not go fishing; for we are always going to have better luck in a few minutes or tomorrow.

From book, Fishing for Fun — and to Wash Your Soul, *by Herbert Hoover, 1963*

. . . There is said to be a tablet of 2000 B.C. which says:

The Gods do not subtract from the allotted span of men's lives the hours spent in fishing.

As further proof that fishing is the Fountain of Youth, I may also cite that many a President of the United States has sought the Fountain of Youth by fishing. . . . Also, fishing reduces the ego in Presidents and former Presidents, for at fishing most men are not equal to boys.

From book, Fishing for Fun — and to Wash Your Soul, *by Herbert Hoover, 1963*

Strong primary instincts — and they are useful instincts — get rejuvenation by a thrust into the simpler life. For instance, we do not catch fish in the presence of, or by the methods of, our vast complex of industrialism, nor in the luxury of summer hotels, nor through higher thought, for that matter. In our outdoor life we get repose from the troubles of soul that this vast complex of civilization imposes upon us in our working hours and our restless nights. Association with the placid ripples of the waves and the quiet chortle of the streams is soothing to our "het-up" anxieties.

From book, Fishing for Fun — and to Wash Your Soul, *by Herbert Hoover, 1963*

This civilization is not going to depend upon what we do when we work so much as what we do in our time off.

The moral and spiritual forces of our country do not lose ground in the hours we are busy on our jobs; their battle is the leisure time. We associate joy with leisure. We have great machinery for joy, some of it destructive, some of it synthetic, some of it mass production. We go to chain theaters and movies; we watch somebody else knock a ball over the fence or kick it over the

goal post. I do that too and I believe in it. I do, however, insist that no organized joy has values comparable to the outdoors. . . . We gain none of the rejuvenating cheer that comes from return to the solemnity, the calm and inspiration of primitive nature.

From book, Fishing for Fun — and to Wash Your Soul, *by Herbert Hoover, 1963*

I am glad to accept this medal on behalf of Herbert, Jr., whose duties as Under Secretary of State have compelled him to be abroad at this time. There is nothing that makes a father's heart glow warmer than accomplishment of his sons. It took me 75 years to achieve such merit as seemed to warrant the Board of Trade to confer this very medal upon me some five years ago. Herbert, Jr., achieved that degree of merit after only 52 years. That you recognize that he is better material than his dad was at that age confirms my own views of him.

Acceptance remarks on behalf of Herbert Hoover, Jr., for the New York Board of Trade Gold Medal, New York, New York, Oct. 13, 1955 (from book, Addresses Upon the American Road 1955-1960)

Shortly after his election to the Presidency, Hoover rode his horse, Billy, in the seclusion of Camp Rapidan, Virginia.

*In our outdoor life we get
repose from the troubles of the soul that
this vast complex of civilization
imposed upon us . . .*

Shamrock Lake in California's Inyo National Forest
is one of the scenic locations in the Hoover Wilderness Area,
named in honor of Herbert Hoover.

E. C. Rockwell, U. S. Forest Service

E. C. Rockwell, U. S. Forest Service

The high altitude seclusion of the Hoover Wilderness Area's Burro Lake (above) provides a sanctuary for many types of wildlife in the Inyo National Forest near Bishop, California. A devoted outdoorsman, Hoover led significant conservation programs while he was President. The Great Smoky Mountains National Park (below) in North Carolina and Tennessee was established in 1930 and contains more than 500,000 acres. Another natural area added during the Hoover administration was Canyon de Chelly National Monument (right) in Arizona. Acquired in 1931, the area encompasses 130 acres of land on the historic Navajo Indian Reservation.

National Park Service

"The true test of civilization is, not the census, nor the size of cities, nor the crops — no, but the kind of man the country turns out."

— RALPH WALDO EMERSON

In my opinion, there has been too much talk about the Common Man. It has been dinned into us that this is the Century of the Common Man. The idea seems to be that the Common Man has come into his own at last.

Thus we are in danger of developing a cult of the Common Man, which means a cult of mediocrity. But there is at least one hopeful sign: I have never been able to find out who this Common Man is. In fact, most Americans, and especially women, will get mad and fight if you try calling them common.

This is hopeful because it shows that most people are holding fast to an essential fact in American life. We believe in equal opportunity for all, but we know that this includes the opportunity to rise to leadership — in other words, to be uncommon.

Let us remember that the great human advances have not been brought about by mediocre men and women. They were brought about by distinctly uncommon people with vital sparks of leadership. Many of the great leaders were, it is true, of humble origin, but that alone was not their greatness.

It is a curious fact that when you get sick you want an uncommon doctor; if your car breaks down you want an uncommonly good mechanic; when we get into war we want dreadfully an uncommon admiral and an uncommon general.

I have never met a father and mother who did not want their children to grow up to be uncommon men and women. May it always be so. For the future of America rests not in mediocrity, but in the constant renewal of leadership in every phase of our national life.

From article, "The Uncommon Man,"
in This Week *magazine, Feb. 6, 1949*
(from book, On Growing Up)

The walnut library room at the
Hoover Memorial Library and Museum at West Branch,
Iowa, contains many of Hoover's personal
memorabilia from his last residence.

Phil McCafferty

by distinctly uncommon people . . .

The Hoover Memorial Library in West Branch, Iowa.

EPILOGUE

Tributes

Mr. Hoover's service to our country, spanning a period of nearly a half-century, was marked by a signal honesty of purpose, a devotion to fundamental principles of ethical conduct, and a deep concern for the welfare of all of his fellow men. Among the rich products of his efforts have been the advancement of the cause of peace, the strengthening of our bonds with other nations, the enrichment of the lives of millions of human beings around the world, and a vital improvement of the operation of this Government. His patriotism knew no partisanship.

A gentle and tolerant man, Mr. Hoover will be long remembered for his humanitarianism, his genuine humility coupled with a determined courage, and the strength of the faith which motivated his actions. He has earned the abiding respect and affection of the people of this nation and other nations throughout the world.

We in this country will be joined by his many friends abroad in mourning the death of this truly dedicated American. But we can take comfort in the inspiring legacy of ideals and example of devotion which he had bequeathed to us all.

PRESIDENT LYNDON B. JOHNSON

The Nation is a loser in the death of President Hoover, one of the most highly respected and revered men of our time. He has by his great service earned the gratitude of America and the free world. Everywhere he was known as a friend of humanity. Mrs. Eisenhower and I join the nation in grieving for the loss of a man who has meant so much to the Republic and to whom we gave our deep affection and admiration.

FORMER PRESIDENT DWIGHT D. EISENHOWER

(Addressed to Mr. Hoover's sons) I was deeply saddened at the passing of your father. He was my good friend and I was his. President Hoover was a devoted public servant and he will be forever remembered for his great humanitarian work. Please express my sympathy to all the family.

FORMER PRESIDENT HARRY S. TRUMAN

President Hoover was one of those rare individuals who lived to hear the overwhelmingly favorable verdict of history on his career. For 60 years he walked proudly with the giants of the earth and in the end he had won the respect and affection of untold millions who are the beneficiaries of his humanitarianism. His name, once vilified by his detractors, will now forever be respected and revered.

FORMER VICE PRESIDENT RICHARD M. NIXON

If anything could assuage the deep sadness of his passing, it is the knowledge that his long life advanced the cause of learning and human dignity and brought relief to human suffering.

WALLACE STERLING, President of Stanford University

Cliff Segerblom

Because he was a man of passion, he made it possible for millions of men, women and children in many lands to live out their lives in health and dignity. Because he was a man of extraordinary intelligence and integrity, he gave our country an example of dedicated leadership which continued long after his time of public office was over. Because he was at heart a scholar and a humanist, his speeches and writings have influenced profoundly the life and thought of our time.

GRAYSON KIRK, President of Columbia University

The late President Hoover was a particular friend of Finland and we among so many other nations cherish his memory as the most warm-hearted statesman this century has brought forth.

PRESIDENT URHO KEKKONEN of Finland

No man of our century saved so many human beings from starvation as he; none gave so many years to public service and political leadership of such a high order and none suffered political calumny with such patience. To all of his almost countless services to his country and to mankind everywhere, he brought the unique touch of greatness as well as the finest moral fiber. This is a better world because Herbert Clark Hoover gave it a lifetime of dedicated service.

FORMER GOVERNOR THOMAS E. DEWEY

The Hoover Dam on the Colorado River touches both Arizona and Nevada. The 726 foot high structure was completed in 1938.

H. J. Evers

An Army honor guard stood a
silent vigil after former President Hoover's
funeral at West Branch, Iowa, in
late October, 1964.

Chronology

1874	Born, August 10, at West Branch, Iowa, of parents Jesse Clark and Hulda Minthorn Hoover.
1885	Moved to Newberg, Oregon, in the family of an uncle after being orphaned at the age of ten. Entered a Quaker secondary school, Pacific Academy, now George Fox College.
1891-1895	Attended Stanford University at Palo Alto, California, and was graduated with a degree in geology and engineering. Worked as a miner and later as an engineering aide in northern California.
1897	Sent to Australia to organize and manage large gold mine.
1898	Became chief engineer, Chinese government mining operations.
1899	Married Miss Lou Henry at Monterey, California. Returned to China with wife and was caught in the Boxer Rebellion.
1901-1914	Acquired and directed worldwide mining interests.
1914-1919	Named chairman of the American Relief Committee, the United States Commission for Relief in Belgium and appointed U.S. Food Administrator.
1919-1921	Led U.S. Relief Commission to feed starving children in defeated nations and Russian relief program. Appointed chairman of the Supreme Economic Council, Interallied Food Council and the Committee on Industrial Relations.
1921-1928	Served as Secretary of Commerce in

Cabinets of Presidents Warren G. Harding and Calvin Coolidge. Published *American Individualism,* 1922.

1928	Nominated by Republican Party for President of the United States, June 14. Elected President defeating New York Governor Alfred E. Smith, November 6.
1929-1933	Inaugurated, March 4, 1929. Stock market collapse plunged the nation into economic depression, October 29, 1929. Organized recovery program of limited government intervention and private voluntary cooperation.
1932	Renominated and defeated by New York Governor Franklin D. Roosevelt, in the Presidential election, November 8.
1934-1942	Published *The Challenge to Liberty, Addresses Upon the American Road, America's First Crusade* and co-authored *The Problems of a Lasting Peace.*
1946-1951	Appointed coordinator of European-Asian-South American food survey and chairman of the first Committee for Reorganization of the Executive Branch of the Federal government by President Harry S. Truman.
1951-1952	Published three volume memoirs.
1953-1955	Named chairman of the second Federal government executive branch reorganization committee by President Dwight D. Eisenhower.
1958	Published *The Ordeal of Woodrow Wilson.*
1964	Died in New York City, October 20, at the age of 90.